bus, Italians have come
largest

P9-BZL-034

THEY CAME FROM ITALY

THEY CAME
FROM ITALY

The Stories of Famous Italian-Americans

By BARBARA MARINACCI

ILLUSTRATED

DODD, MEAD & COMPANY

NEW YORK

In memory of my husband's father

MICHAEL ANGELO MARINACCI—

a proud Italian
a good American

Library of Congress Catalog Card Number: 67-12949
Printed in the United States of America
by The Cornwall Press, Inc., Cornwall, N. Y.

Contents

Contents

Illustrations

Following page 86

GUIDE TO PRONUNCIATION OF NAMES

Henri de Tonti .... ahn-REE deh TONE-tee
Filippo Mazzei .... fee-LEE-poh maht-TSAY-ee
Constantino Brumidi .... kon-stan-TEE-noh broo-MEE-dee
Luigi Palma di Cesnola ....
                 loo-EE-gee PAHL-mah dee chez-NOH-lah
Francesca Cabrini ....frahn-CHEZ-kah kah-BREE-nee
Arturo Toscanini .... ahr-TOO-roh toh-skah-NEE-nee
Amadeo Giannini .... ah-mah-DAY-oh jah-NEE-nee
Fiorello La Guardia .... fee-oh-REL-loh lah GWAR-dee-ah
Enrico Fermi .... ehn-REE-koh FEHR-mee

MAP OF ITALY

KEY TO BIRTHPLACES

1. Henri de Tonti
2. Philip Mazzei
3. Constantino Brumidi
4. Luigi Palma di Cesnola
5. Francesca Cabrini
6. Arturo Toscanini
7. A. P. Giannini's parents
8F. Fiorello La Guardia's father
8M. Fiorello La Guardia's mother
9. Enrico Fermi

An Introduction

The Italians Come

"I love Thee, Italy, my native land . . . I love Thee,
America, with manhood's strong love . . ."

WHEN THE ITALIAN NAVIGATOR Christopher Columbus
sailed westward across the vast, uncharted Atlantic Ocean
almost five hundred years ago and discovered a New World,
he started the great migration from Europe. Each group that
came to North America—whether Spanish conquistadors, English settlers, French fur traders, Negro slaves, or the waves of
immigrants from Germany, Ireland, Italy, and other European countries—brought a special heritage. The United States
was shaped by these peoples—long-established or newly arrived—with their many different needs and interests.

During the centuries of the colonization of the Americas,
Italy founded no colonies. Not until 1860 did Italy become a
unified and independent nation. Before then, *Italia* was only
the name for the long, boot-shaped peninsula in southern
Europe that jutted out into the Mediterranean Sea and was
divided into a patchwork of kingdoms, duchies, and city-
states, that feuded among themselves and, when their power

1

waned, were conquered and ruled by their stronger European neighbors.

Italians wishing to go abroad frequently served foreign countries. Experienced seafarers, they often made bold sea captains. Spain benefited from Columbus's quest for a new route to Asia. Giovanni Caboto of Venice, called John Cabot, sailed in English ships along the coast of North America. The Florentine pilot Amerigo Vespucci, voyaging for Spain and Portugal, determined that the new lands were not adjuncts to Asia but whole continents to themselves, thus causing an early sixteenth-century map maker to name this terrain "America." An Italian navigator in the service of France, Giovanni da Verrazano, was the first European to enter the New York harbor.

The Italians who came afterwards, to explore and settle in these lands, went as individuals, not in groups: adventurers seeking fortunes, soldiers, dedicated missionaries, educated men desiring religious or political freedom, or skilled craftsmen whose work would be welcomed in frontier communities. Some worked for Spain or France; others dwelled in the English settlements along the eastern edge of North America. These first Italian immigrants fitted easily into the prevailing society.

When the United States was formed, there were at least several hundred Italian families settled in the first thirteen states. (It is believed that William Paca, one of the signers of the Declaration of Independence, had an Italian ancestry.) Their professions were usually family-acquired trades like glass blowing, stonecutting, cobbling, weaving, and farming. Some, of course, were doctors, merchants, lawyers, teachers, musicians, and portraitists. Primarily from northern or central Italy, they were often escaping political or religious oppression in their home provinces; economic betterment was only a secondary factor in their emigration.

During the middle decades of the nineteenth century, as the industrial revolution took hold, the nature of immigration to America changed. In Europe many people were being displaced from the land or from their trades. There seemed to be land and work enough for them in the United States. Large groups of immigrants, especially from Ireland and Germany, arrived to help the rapidly expanding and developing United States cut down forests, lay out farmlands, dig canals, construct railroads. Towns grew into great cities throbbing with factories; the cities needed tall buildings, paved streets, gas and water mains, sewers, streetcar tracks, tunnels, bridges. Coal and iron mines required a steady supply of cheap labor. Railroads were being built to join farmlands to cities, factory and mining towns to ports—so that finally the whole nation was spanned. Most of these jobs still had to be done by human hands. Though the work was hard and the wages small, immigrants eager to make good in the new land were willing to tackle the backbreaking jobs.

Italian laborers, long employed in construction projects elsewhere in Europe, were accustomed to working and living abroad for a time. Now from the faraway United States of America the call went out for more "pick-and-shovel" men. It resounded throughout southern Italy and Sicily and was heard by hundreds of thousands of farm workers barely able to feed their families by tilling the parched, worn-out, rocky land belonging to absentee landlords. They also heard rumors that gold lay in the very streets of America, dropped by people so rich they could not be bothered to pick it up; yet even the promise of daily wages seemed like gold to the Italian peasants, the *contadini*.

Italian-American agents for steamship or railroad companies or from growing industries busily recruited them. The new steamships had shortened the Atlantic voyage from several months to less than two weeks, thereby reducing the high mortality rate and terrible discomfort in the crowded steerage class. A would-be emigrant felt less fearful of going to America if some of his townspeople were already there to greet him; and he knew he could find a *padrone,* an Italian boss who would watch over him on the job—the payment for his services being a portion of the wages. (Later on, in America, as his debt to his *padrone* seemed ever to mount, he would question the ethics of the *padrone* system.)

For the poor of Italy, America meant a new beginning. Saving or borrowing enough money for their fares, the *contadini* and the jobless city dwellers poured into the United States ports at the rate of several thousand per day. Hard-working, adaptable, easygoing, and thrifty, with little need for luxuries, they were welcomed by many industries. Sometimes they worked for a few years and then returned to their homeland; but most of them stayed and, to fulfill their need for family life, sent for relatives, married, and had children who were born United States citizens.

The great wave of Italian immigration to the United States began in the last two decades of the nineteenth century and continued through the first two decades of the twentieth. In all, close to five million Italians came to the United States after 1830 (when immigration figures began to be recorded)—a total exceeded only by the Germans, whose influx was not so concentrated in time. Well over half of these Italian immigrants became American citizens. They and their children now make up about 14 per cent (the highest percentage) of the foreign-stock population in the United States.

Usually dwelling in city tenements close to their work, the Italian immigrants created "Little Italies," nearly self-sufficient colonies with their own stores and churches and amusement places, even Italian-language newspapers. (Until recently the Italian-stock population in New York City alone was larger than that of Rome.) These colonies, partially separating the Italians from American society, gave them a sense of protection from dangers known and unknown, and sometimes imparted the feeling of still dwelling in Italy. Consequently, many Italians living there were not readily "Americanized." Those who settled in small towns and rural communities were usually assimilated more rapidly and effectively into the mainstream of American life.

Often it was the immigrants' children who provided the link between the Old World and the New. Taught in American schools, learning English early, and venturing into the area outside the Italian district, they brought America back into their parents' lives; frequently, however, there were painful conflicts between the two generations, whose outlooks were so divergent. In the United States most of the young people enjoyed far better opportunities than they would have had in Italy, where schooling was brief, if at all, for the lower classes, and a career was usually confined to a family's trade and social rank.

The many Italians who became proud citizens of their new country increasingly participated in its civic life and devised numerous ways to make their private life more congenial. Opportunities and challenges caused them to discover new talents and possibilities; sorrows and setbacks revealed heretofore hidden depths and strengths. The American experience widened the Italian immigrant's horizon and matured him. Yet often he looked back nostalgically to Italy, the land of his birth and childhood, which held his earliest and fondest memories. He dreamed and talked of returning there some-day to finish out his years; but he rarely went back to stay. His work, his home, his family, and his friends were now in America.

When the immigrant became a United States citizen, his primary national allegiance shifted. "I love Thee, Italy, my native land, with that mystic love with which men turn to their native country and as pilgrims to their shrine," wrote the young sociologist Constantine Panunzio after facing a difficult decision as to his future abode. "I love Thee, America, with manhood's strong love, born out of the unfolding of the mind, the evolving of the soul, the sufferings and joys, the toil and the larger loves of the years." Like most other immigrants from Italy, he chose to remain in America.

Although 85 per cent of the incoming Italians named agriculture as their trade, a survey made of them during the 1920s revealed that only 15 per cent were working as farmers in the United States. Most of the *contadini* had settled in large cities or industrial towns close to the port of entry and were working in factories or doing heavy labor. If they did manage to save enough money to start their own businesses, they usually saw greater profit or convenience in leasing or buying city property rather than running a farm. They opened grocery stores and barber shops, operated shoeshine concerns, bought tenement buildings, or contracted for city work like collecting trash or laying down asphalt.

But many Italians did manage to return to the land, to work on farms and often to buy their own. The time of the government's public land grants had passed; anyway, the Italian farmers preferred already cleared and settled land. They usually took over and revived overworked or abandoned acreage, achieving veritable marvels through a basic understanding of soil and its produce as well as a capacity for hard work.

Yet however hard he worked and whatever he accomplished, the Italian-American for many years was considered a "second-class citizen" by other people. Coming as a group late upon the American scene and then, seemingly, all in a rush, Italians inevitably encountered accommodation problems—and outright prejudice. Like other national or ethnic groups before and after them, they were given insulting slang names: "Wop," "Dago," and "Guinea." ("Wop" probably originated in the Neapolitan dialect word *guappo*—a flashy, show-off fellow—which southern Italians at first used to describe some of their own members. "Dago" must have come from the Spanish name Diego, which Americans trimmed and for a while applied to anybody of obvious Latin or Mediterranean origin. "Guinea" or "Ginney" perhaps derived from an earlier English reference to the dark-skinned natives of British Guiana; taken up by Americans, it was bestowed upon the swarthy, dark-eyed Italian newcomers.)

There may be an almost instinctive reaction on people's parts to a stranger in their midst whose language, appearance, behavior, and religious practices are different from their own. Since the United States had long been receiving immigrants from many lands, Americans should have been more gracious in accepting these differences, less fearful of the effects of welcoming aliens into their midst who would, in time, fit admirably into the culture. A good many Americans were, after all, themselves the offspring of recent immigrants. But just as many had felt threatened by the German and Irish "invasions," now they worried about Italians, who resembled the native American stock even less. All Italians were reduced to a single stereotype of the "dark foreigner" who was ignorant and ill-washed and noisy, smelled of garlic and wine, spoke a funny kind of pidgin English by adding Italianate terminal vowels to many words, possessed a strong singing voice but an explosive temper, and doubtless was plotting some terrible crime. Invariably, this stereotyped Italian worked at a job that elicited little respect: he was an organ-grinder, fishmonger, stevedore, bootblack, or pushcart vendor. Furthermore, it was somehow decided that he came from inferior racial stock and that he and his children could never become suitable American citizens. To complicate the situation further, Italians divided themselves into northern and southern branches, disputing the merits and defects of each.

To offset the insidious effects of intolerance upon their self-esteem, Italians joined together in fraternal organizations like the Order of the Sons of Italy in America. Understandably, they took great pride in the fact that their predecessor Columbus had begun the emigration from Europe—from which many Americans now apparently wanted them excluded. They reminded themselves and their children, too, that Italy was the birthplace of such remarkable men as St. Thomas Aquinas, Michelangelo, Da Vinci, Raphael, Dante, Galileo, Garibaldi, Verdi, Caruso, and Marconi.

The scorned Italians in America could also recall that their homeland had produced several glorious periods in the history of mankind. The Roman Empire twenty centuries before had exercised a powerful civilizing force throughout the Western world, and its language, Latin, echoed in the modern European tongues and survived in jurisprudence and the Catholic Church. Christianity had taken its official seat in Rome; and when barbarian hordes overran Italy during the Dark Ages, the Church preserved much of the learning and artistry of the ancient Greeks and Romans. This classical heritage, brought to light, inspired the Renaissance, a new birth of the human spirit originating in Italy and producing a flowering of the arts, sciences, and philosophy which spread throughout medieval Europe, ultimately to structure the modern world.

But no matter what the Italian-Americans said or did to prove their intrinsic worth, prejudice against them and other immigrant groups still proliferated. Many people wanted immigration to be limited. During the 1920s, Congress began to impose a series of annual quotas on immigrants allowed into the United States. This National Origins Quota System, reflecting the widespread prejudice in the country, was purposely set up to halt the "new immigration" from southern and eastern Europe, while giving continued encouragement to the "preferred stock," the "old immigration" from northern and western Europe. The result was that the high quotas for England, Ireland, Germany, and the Scandinavian countries were rarely filled, whereas a backlog of immigration applications for the 5,666 annual quota from Italy grew close to 150,000.

Happily, times have changed. As the Italian immigrants and their offspring were integrated into American society far more effectively than most people had imagined possible, and as their worthy contributions became increasingly apparent, the unreasoning fear of the Italian in our midst largely departed. Through education, books, movies, and jet-age travel, many Americans are rapidly becoming Italophiles.

In 1965, an enlightened attitude toward immigrant groups resulted in the passage by Congress of a new Immigration Bill. Although retaining an over-all quota on entries, it eliminated the offensive and discriminatory national-origins restrictions and instead gave preference to prospective immigrants of any European nation with established family connections in America or with special skills useful in the United States.

Among Italian-Americans today, some are foreign-born but most are second- or even third-generation Americans; and of these, a sizable portion are only fractionally Italian. No longer are we surprised to encounter an Italian name in a captain of industry, a renowned scientist, an educational leader, an ingenious designer, an eminent doctor, a brilliant lawyer, a superb musician, a shrewd financier. Benefiting from good educations, the opportunity to pursue any career, and freedom from prejudice, Italian-Americans now freely lend their talent and energy to American life. Americans all, there may yet remain a trace of an inherent Italian spirit, which may be a key to their success.

Italians generally are a people with strong feelings usually much in evidence; they rarely hide or dissimulate affection, interest, grief, anger. Their love—for children, parents, friends, and land, for all things beautiful and useful—is warm and tangible. They are intensely proud; and they are greatly loyal to people and things close to them. Italians rarely do things timidly, by half-measures; body and soul seem joined in work and in pleasure. Life is lived, dramatically, to the hilt, whether in joy or sorrow. They labor long and hard, taking delight in doing a task well; and when work is done, they relax wholly and enjoyably. (Significantly, Italians in both Italy and the United States suffer far less than most other groups from heart disease, alcoholism, mental illness, and suicide—all barometers telling of deep emotional distress.)

Certain Italian words have found special favor among Americans. *Paesano*—fellow-countryman—has become synonymous with "pal." *Vino* is an affectionate name for wine shared among friends. *Bambino* is known by almost everyone as "baby." The English vocabulary has long contained many Italian or Italian-derived words: motto, propaganda, quota, fiasco, incognito, ballot, contraband, replica, virtuoso, gusto, confetti, dilettante, manifesto, altruism, ballerina, umbrella, scenario, influenza, malaria, extravaganza, lava, volcano, inferno—to name a few.

Innumerable words relating to the arts are directly traceable to the paramount contributions of Italy during the Renaissance period. Since in Italy music was set to an orderly seven-tone scale and was given its first system of notation, the vocabulary of music—an international language—is largely Italian: opera, soprano, coloratura, basso, falsetto, solo, oratorio, libretto, tempo, finale, and so forth. Musical instruments designed in Italy have Italian names: piano, viola, piccolo, trombone, timpani. "Sonnet" comes from the Italian *sonnetta,* devised by Petrarch; other literary terms dating back to the Renaissance are stanza, simile, terza rima. Italy as the "cradle" of the fine arts is displayed in the Italian origins of many words in painting, sculpture, and architecture: studio, tempera, fresco, mural, torso, cameo, terra cotta, portico, cupola, campanile, stucco. Also, since many Renaissance Italians served abroad as soldiers, familiar military terms in English came originally from the Italian: battalion, brigade, cavalry, regiment, artillery, infantry, corporal, captain, general. Our standard banking methods originated in Italy's lively mercantile cities. The word "bank" itself comes from the Italian *banca*—the bench or table at which money-changers operated.

Bravo to cheer a good performance is a near-universal exclamation. The word "pants" came from Pantalone, the popular *commedia dell' arte* character whose distinctive trousers or "pantaloons" made for a long time a topic for international jokes. The slanting printing type known as "italic" was created by a Venetian printer. "Jeans," the uniform of American youth, got their name from a blue-denim cloth first made in Genoa. A "milliner" was called so because Milan was once famous for its hatmakers. Early pistols were manufactured in Pistoia. Venetian blinds were first popular in Venice; Roman candles were produced in Rome. Baloney—as a prepared meat or as slang now for "nonsense"—came from the type of salami made in Bologna. Sardines were caught off the coast of Sardinia; the cantaloupe was first grown in the Italian town Cantalupo; the familiar Neapolitan ice cream, in colored layers, resembles *spumone* made in Naples.

In the United States, Italian foodstuffs were popular even among the nation's founding fathers; today they occupy more and more space on supermarket shelves. There are few American towns without some kind of Italian restaurant, and cities may have a dozen or more, from pizza parlors featuring the American-style variation on the popular Neapolitan dinner pie, to luxury-class gourmet establishments. A popular enterprise too is the "espresso house," an informal gathering place for students, artists, and talkers, who sit for hours—reading, sketching, writing or reciting poetry, or arguing—while sipping steam-machine-made *caffè espresso*. Recipes for Italian food specialties abound in American cookbooks. Everybody is familiar with Italian *pasta,* especially macaroni and spaghetti—basically an Oriental foodstuff introduced in Italy by Marco Polo. Italian cheeses—parmesan, romano, gorgonzola, ricotta, mozzarella, provolone, Bel Paese—have become standard stock in our grocery stores. Salami has long been a regular item in the American diet.

Italians popularized the use of the tomato in both its fresh and cooked forms; a vegetable native to the Americas, it was long considered poisonous by northern Europeans. Among the vegetables well-liked by Italians are broccoli, zucchini, eggplant, bell pepper, and the artichoke; at first grown on Italian truck farms for Italian-American consumption, they are now indispensable produce commodities. The popularity of wine in the United States is also traceable to the Italian-Americans who planted many vineyards large and small in favorable locations, especially in California. Their most dependable early customers were their own people, who preferred wine to the stronger, distilled spirits.

The map of the United States has numerous Italian place names. Tontitown, Arkansas, was founded by a group of Italian immigrant farmers led by a priest, who named their town after the early Italian explorer Henri de Tonti. Towns scattered across America honor illustrious Italians of the past—Columbus, Dante, Cavour, Garibaldi, Verdi. Many states contain towns named by nostalgic immigrants or admiring native-born Americans after famous Italian cities: Rome, Naples, Venice, Florence, Turin, Genoa, Parma. Other towns and names for geographical features are descriptively Italian, like Montebello and Roseto.

This book tells the life stories of nine Italians who lived in the United States. Since their lives spanned almost three centuries, through them the larger story of the Italian emigration to America can frequently be glimpsed. Seven of the subjects were born in Italy. The other two—Giannini and La Guardia—were born in the United States of Italian immigrant parents, and their life work was closely involved with the Italian-American community. All but two of the nine people—Tonti and Toscanini—were United States citizens.

These nine people were very different from each other in origin, personality, interests, and profession. Yet all had this in common: they were highly energetic and intensely involved in bringing to fulfillment in America some dream or ideal, a search for knowledge or perfection, or a practical contribution to society. They all worked hard, sometimes with an almost single-minded dedication, to achieve their special goals; some only partially succeeded; the others never considered themselves finished in their quests or self-appointed missions. They aimed high—and accomplished much. Their inspired capacity for doing, for work, perhaps best characterizes too their many countrymen who came to America, stayed and worked, and who had children who have also worked in thousands of ways to build and shape our nation.

A final chapter mentions other Italian-Americans who have figured in American life.

An Iron Hand in the Wilderness

Henri de Tonti

> "He is the man who best knows these regions; he has twice gone down to the sea; he has been far inland to the most remote tribes, and is beloved and feared everywhere."

THE BEST-KNOWN and most admirable of the early Italian settlers in North America was The Man with the Iron Hand: Henri de Tonti. A hundred years before the United States was born, he came to America to assist the French explorer La Salle in his adventures. For the rest of his life, for a quarter-century, Tonti roved through the wilderness that was his home—a vast territory now parcelled out into a dozen states. Tonti traveled through forests and over mountains, across plains and upon rivers unseen before by white men. And while exploring, fur trading, pacifying or fighting Indians, building ships or forts, managing trading posts, and founding settlements, Tonti displayed a catalog of virtues that made him the best representative possible of European civilization.

He was named Enrico Tonti at his birth, probably in 1650 at Gaeta, where his father was governor. After taking part in a brief, ill-fated rebellion against southern Italy's Spanish rulers, Lorenzo Tonti fled to France with his family. A clever financier, he was welcomed at the French court by a fellow Italian, Cardinal Mazarin, young Louis XIV's chief adviser. There Lorenzo Tonti introduced a novel life-insurance plan still known as the "tontine."

Enrico—whose name was Frenchified to Henri de Tonti (or Tonty)—joined the French navy as a youthful cadet and eventually became a captain. During a battle with Spain, a grenade shattered his right hand. Henri grasped his sword with the other hand and made a sharp cut through the bone. When his arm healed, Tonti attached a metal hand, which in the New World would become legendary. With it he could ply a canoe paddle, clean a fish, stir up the embers of a campfire. It also proved "good medicine," inspiring awe and obedience from troublemakers. The Indians thought that The Man with the Iron Hand possessed mysterious, superhuman powers; when he talked, they listened with respect.

When Tonti's naval company was disbanded in 1678, he looked in Paris for new employment. The Prince of Conti, a family friend, told him about an ambitious explorer who was collecting men and supplies for a big venture in North America: to travel the length of the Mississippi River, from the Great Lakes down to the sea, and claim all the lands he passed through for the King of France.

Robert Cavelier, the Sieur de la Salle, needed a good lieutenant to assist him in New France. When he met Tonti, he saw a lean man in his late twenties whose mustache, waxed carefully at the tips, curled upward toward calm and intelligent dark eyes. Looking at his slender frame and that heavy metal hand, La Salle doubted that the Italian could survive the rigors of the American wilderness. But La Salle liked

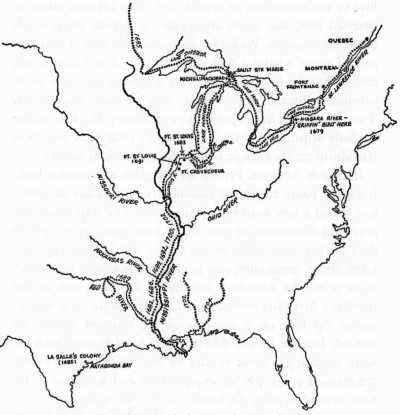

Tonti's travels in North America

Tonti and took a chance on him. It was probably the most fortunate decision he ever made. For a decade Tonti would serve him faithfully and capably. Between the stalwart but easygoing Italian and the ambitious but introverted Frenchman a close bond grew, which sustained them through innumerable hardships.

To his followers, La Salle seemed remote, rigid, demanding. If he commanded fear and respect, he did not call forth love or understanding or loyalty; too often his men failed or deserted him. But Tonti always gave a human touch to his leader's endeavors. While La Salle issued orders, Tonti persuaded men; what La Salle commenced, Tonti completed; and though La Salle had the great dreams, Tonti gave them substance. Idealist and realist, they needed each other. Through Tonti, in the perspective of history, the formidable La Salle acquired a heart. The story of their aims and their friendship makes a tragic tale in early American history.

In North America, French and English adventurers looking for a route across the continent to the riches of China had found a new source of wealth: furs. The important geographical discoveries in New Spain were made by conquistadors lusting after gold; in the cooler north, men explored lakes, rivers, mountains, and plains as they sought the beaver skins prized by European merchants. La Salle, one of the frontier's first "big businessmen," had thought of a way to gather up furs on a grand scale. It was not money he wanted. Instead, he had a bright dream—of France, with his help, founding a great empire in the very heart of North America. To pay for his explorations and settlements, La Salle needed to make his fortune in the fur trade.

During the two-month voyage to New France, La Salle unfolded his plans to Tonti. First of all, they would build the first sailing ship on the Great Lakes, a large vessel that could carry to the hinterlands whole crews of *coureurs de bois* ("woods runners")—the rowdy, rough-living, fur-trading agents who lived among the Indians and swapped metal tools, cloth, blankets, pots, guns, trinkets, and brandy for beaver pelts—and return swiftly and safely across the interconnected upper lakes with cargoes of furs. No longer, then, would La Salle's fur packets have to travel down to the Montreal market in *voyageurs'* canoes, which were easily swamped in storms and prey to predatory Indians and rival fur traders.

The ship built, La Salle and Tonti would then erect a fort and trading post along the Illinois River, there to build a second large ship that would take them down the Mississippi to its mouth, completing the trip that Father Marquette and Louis Jolliet had made in 1673—which was halted halfway but still indicated that the great river flowed not into the Pacific (as the French had hoped) but into the Gulf of Mexico. La Salle believed that if the river did go southward, it could be used profitably by fur traders throughout the year—unlike the St. Lawrence which, though it gave the French a unique water route penetrating into the continent over a thousand miles, was frozen during the long northern winters. Developing a strong network of settlements stretching along the length of the Mississippi would enable the French to dominate the heartland and, ultimately, much of North America. It was a dream of empire that was grandiose yet practical.

La Salle and Tonti arrived at Quebec in September of 1678. There Tonti met New France's governor, Count Frontenac, whose vision of future French power in the New World resembled his friend La Salle's. In Quebec, Tonti began mustering men for the work ahead. "His honorable character and his amiable disposition were well known to you," La Salle wrote gratefully to the Prince of Conti; "but perhaps you would not have thought him capable of doing things for which a strong constitution, an acquaintance with the country, and the use of both hands seemed absolutely necessary. Nevertheless, his energy and address make him equal to anything."

After voyaging up the St. Lawrence River, Tonti and La

Salle passed through Montreal, the bustling center of the fur
trade. Then, on Lake Ontario, they stopped at Fort Frontenac, built by the governor and La Salle several years before.
This first fort in the Iroquois-dominated territory brought
French military power to the Northwest and made a strong
and accessible trading post for friendly Indian tribes. But it
had also caused bitter jealousy among rival fur traders. Fearing that Frontenac and La Salle were establishing a commercial monopoly, they tried to defeat their every move.

In a vessel laden with supplies, La Salle's party now sailed
across Lake Ontario, landing at the mouth of the Niagara
River. La Salle's eloquence gained the Indians' reluctant
permission to build a large "wooden canoe" upon the Niagara, above the thundering falls only recently discovered by
the Europeans. While La Salle and Tonti were choosing a
place for their shipyard, their supply ship was wrecked on the
shore below—perhaps a bad omen. Having to return to Fort
Frontenac for new equipment, La Salle confidently left Tonti
in charge of building his ship.

Tonti had a crew of thirty workmen, plus a few soldiers
and a priest named Father Hennepin. First, they built a small
fort. Then in the bitter cold they began cutting wood for the
forty-five-ton vessel. Since food rations were low and the
work was hard, the carpenters grumbled and threatened to
leave. Tonti told them to proceed with their jobs—or else
find their own way back to civilization. The work went on.

As the ship grew tall on its dry dock, the suspicious and
envious Iroquois came to study it, standing like sullen, silent
shadows in the distance. Learning to deal firmly and cautiously with the Indians, Tonti kept a constant guard on both
camp and ship. Under his supervision the vessel was nearly
finished by early spring. Men went down below Niagara Falls

to carry up the equipment that La Salle had sent to them. Finally the *Griffin*—named after the mythical beast on Frontenac's coat of arms—was ready for her launching. Father Hennepin bestowed his blessing, the assembled workers cheered heartily, then pushed the *Griffin* into the river while the Indian spectators gaped in wonderment.

Tonti must have been proud of his backwoods masterwork, this first sailing ship on the upper Great Lakes. Sixty feet long, with a raised quarter-deck, two large square sails, a griffin carved on her prow, and five cannons, she lay on the river, awaiting her master's return.

Summer was almost over when La Salle came back. His new ship, proof of Tonti's trustworthiness and the first important piece in his plan, helped him bear his ill fortune. His enemies had persuaded some of his creditors that he had embarked on a foolhardy venture; much of his property had been seized as security against their loans. By gathering up furs from his coureurs de bois dispatched the year before, La Salle's *Griffin* would help him pay his debts at once.

Autumn was touching the woods along Lake Erie as they started out. The *Griffin*'s sails caught gentle winds; she passed through the Detroit River and tiny Lake St. Clair. After entering Lake Huron, the ship was tossed around by a sudden storm as though she were only a bark canoe, setting her passengers to praying. When the squall departed as quickly as it had come, they crossed Lake Huron and came to St. Ignace of Michillimackinac, the settlement at the straits connecting the three upper lakes. There Jesuit priests, voyageurs, and Indians streamed down to the harbor to see the wonderful sight—a real sailing ship that dwarfed the hundred canoes like a whale among perches.

Learning that some of his coureurs had cheated him, La

Salle sent Tonti off to Sault Ste. Marie to arrest a group there. They were to meet later at the St. Joseph River, on the southern tip of Lake Michigan, and from there head southward to the Illinois River—to build a fort and the second sailing ship.

La Salle now took the *Griffin* into Lake Michigan, picked up furs waiting for him and, with misgivings, entrusted his ship with its cargo of beaver skins to the pilot and a small crew and sent them back to the Niagara with a long list of supplies to bring back from Fort Frontenac. As his party then set out to rendezvous with Tonti, a fierce autumn storm swamped their canoes and drove them to shore. For the next weeks wind and rain rarely abated. Wet, famished, exhausted, harassed by Indians, La Salle and his men finally reached the St. Joseph—but Tonti was not there.

For almost a month La Salle waited for his Italian lieutenant, occupying his restless, complaining men by building a small fort. Finally Tonti and his followers straggled in, victims too of the miserable weather. But there was still no sign of the *Griffin's* sails, though it was past time for her return.

La Salle could wait no longer. Winter was coming, food was already scarce, and the rivers would soon freeze over. In early December the company ascended the St. Joseph, carried their eight canoes over to the Kankakee, and made their way down it to the Illinois River. Passing through the winter-brown rushes of the prairie country, they came at last to the Illinois tribe's winter quarters. La Salle told the Indians that he wanted to build a fort in their territory which would protect them from their hated enemies, the Iroquois. He also wished to make a boat which would travel all the way down the Mississippi and then return with gifts for them. Although La Salle's oratory temporarily swayed them, the

Illinois later changed their minds and warned him that the Mississippi had impassable rapids and terrible monsters.

In the winter of 1680, Fort Crèvecoeur ("Heartbreak") was built and the new ship started. Since the ship needed the equipment that the *Griffin* was to deliver at the St. Joseph, La Salle left Crèvecoeur under Tonti's command and with five men set off toward the northeast, to discover the reason for the *Griffin's* delay in coming. He had begun to fear the worst. For two months he pushed across the frozen land. Coming at last to his fort on the Niagara, La Salle got two numbing blows: the *Griffin* had never reached there with her precious cargo, so doubtless was sunk; a ship from France carrying more men and supplies for La Salle's Mississippi expedition had been wrecked along the St. Lawrence.

Other men confronting such catastrophes, beset by rivals, and struggling beneath a crushing burden of debts, would have given up by now. But La Salle was buoyed up by his vision of a Mississippi empire. Scarcely pausing for rest, he set off to Montreal, where he somehow obtained new credit for his venture. While gathering men and supplies, he received a hurried message from his Italian lieutenant, who told of the mutiny of the men at Crèvecoeur while Tonti was away. The rebels had destroyed Crèvecoeur and carried off whatever they could; now only Tonti, two friars, and three other men remained.

La Salle had but one hope now: that Tonti had saved the forge and other tools for finishing the ship. Though all else had gone awry, they must at least make the Mississippi journey. Hurrying off to join Tonti, La Salle learned that the Iroquois were on the warpath and heading toward the Illinois. He quickened his pace, but when he reached the Illinois River, he saw that the Iroquois had preceded him.

The Indian town lay in ruins, though its inhabitants had escaped. Continuing on, he came to Fort Crèvecoeur, where the buildings and fortifications were charred wrecks. Yet there was the half-completed boat, with its ribs poking dismally up at the sky. On a side plank a mutineer had scrawled, "We are all savages." The Iroquois had touched the ship only to remove nails.

There was no sign of Tonti and his companions. Farther down the river La Salle found a meadow where the invaders had finally slaughtered some Illinois—but all their victims were women and children whose protecting warriors had fled. La Salle was disgusted and disturbed. Had Tonti been killed too? Was he a captive of the Iroquois or of the Illinois? Or had he somehow managed to escape both tribes?

With a lingering hope that his brave Tonti still lived, La Salle followed the river and finally came to that spot he had hoped to reach at a happier time—the juncture of the Illinois River with the mighty Mississippi. But La Salle could not take the long journey now; he must wait for another year, for more men, for adequate supplies. And then, if miracles happened, Tonti would come too. La Salle returned upstream, wanting to reach his St. Joseph fort before winter set in. Along the Kankakee he saw wood cut by an iron hatchet. Hope surged in him: surely it was a sign that Tonti had passed by while returning north to some outpost of civilization.

While wintering in his small St. Joseph fort and recovering from snow blindness, La Salle heard that Tonti was indeed alive and safe. In the spring of 1681 the two friends met at Michillimackinac, where Tonti told La Salle of his own adventures.

Tonti and his five companions had lived with the Illinois

at their summer lake town while waiting for La Salle. They had saved the heavy forge and the other tools. But when the Iroquois came, the Illinois, accusing the Frenchmen of planning the attack, made prisoners of their guests, proposed terrible tortures, and hurled the irreplaceable forge into the river.

Tonti had tried to mediate. Braving bullets and arrows from both tribes and holding aloft a wampum belt as a sign of truce, he crossed to the Iroquois camp. Swarthy and partly dressed like an Illinois, he was surrounded at once by frenzied young warriors, one of whom stabbed at his heart but hit a rib instead. Then they noticed that their victim did not have pierced ears—so he must be a Frenchman, as he claimed. The bleeding Tonti demanded that the Iroquois leave the Illinois—"the children of the King of France"—in peace.

Tonti told his captors that it was folly for them to fight, since the Illinois had 1,200 warriors, and sixty Frenchmen with guns to back them up. The Iroquois grew more respectful and finally released Tonti, who staggered back into the arms of Father Zenobe Membre.

Setting fire to their lodges, the Illinois departed, and the Iroquois then occupied the town. Tonti's boasts of Illinois strength had made them uneasy, so they asked him to negotiate a truce with their adversaries. Too eagerly the Illinois agreed to stop fighting. And when a callow hostage unwittingly revealed that his people had only 500 warriors—and not even six Frenchmen, by now—the Iroquois were furious at Tonti's deception. "I had much difficulty in getting out of the scrape," he admitted.

Tonti had done all he could to save the weak Illinois from their bloodthirsty foes. Driven from the Iroquois camp, he and his men headed northward, in a leaky canoe. Father Ribourde was murdered by savages as he prayed in solitude. Their only food was the wild garlic they dug from the ground, and a few parched vegetables. Finally, their spirits flagging and their bodies weakened by cold, hunger, and continuous traveling, they were found by friendly Indians, who took them to a winter haven at Green Bay.

Now, in the spring of 1681, Tonti and La Salle were together again, ready to face more ordeals. La Salle was still determined to go down the Mississippi to the sea, and they spent the summer at Fort Frontenac, collecting men and supplies for the journey. La Salle abandoned the plan of building a large sturdy ship for the trip; he would rely instead upon the fragile but easily built canoes.

At December's end, the twenty-three Frenchmen and thirty-one Indians in La Salle's expedition left Lake Michigan, dragged their canoes up the frozen Chicago river (where one day a great city would stand), and made their way to the Illinois, which flowed freely and bore their canoes for three hundred miles. On February 6, 1682, they came to the Mississippi. La Salle and Tonti must have greeted with joy and relief the river that would draw them down to new triumphs and dangers.

Soon after setting off, they saw a wide, muddy, roiling river entering the Mississippi from the west; it was the Missouri. By mid-March, as they reached the Arkansas River, the air had warmed. The party met gentle Indians who gave them a feast in a land that was beautiful and fertile. When Tonti expressed his pleasure in the place, La Salle granted him it as his seignory. (It was already an historic spot. There in 1542 the Spanish conquistador De Soto had died of a fever; and there in 1673 Marquette and Jolliet had stopped their journey down the Mississippi.)

Traveling several hundred miles farther, La Salle halted at a swamp and sent Tonti and Father Membre inland to visit the great town of the Taensas Indians. Tonti was impressed with their well-built houses of sun-baked mud and straw, and fascinated by the people's respect for their ruler, believed to be a descendant of the Sun God. "Their chiefs are held in as much consideration as our kings," Tonti reported. After an exchange of gifts, the Europeans continued their journey.

One day they encountered a canoe full of Indians, and Tonti's crew pursued it, to be suddenly threatened by a hundred warriors on the shore. Tonti sped back to La Salle, but later returned and held up a peace pipe, to proffer friendship. The Natchez invited the Frenchmen to visit their settlement—where La Salle planted a large cross that bore the French arms. The Indians were flattered, little suspecting that the gift claimed their land for the King of France.

They were not far now from their journey's end. The land became flat and swampy; the river was deeper, narrower, meandering; some could smell the sea. On April 6, they came to a marshy section where the Mississippi split into three channels. Tonti's crew took the middle steam as three parties separated and set off through brackish, swirling water. Soon all emerged upon the sea: the Gulf of Mexico, which the Spanish said belonged to them. The travelers then reassembled on dry ground just above the river's right channel. There on the bank La Salle prepared a column with the French arms. Upon it was inscribed: "Louis the Great, King of France and Ruler of Navarre—the 9th of April, 1682."

In a solemn ceremony led by Father Membre the *Te Deum* was chanted, the men joyously shouted *Vive le Roi*, and La

Salle planted the column that proclaimed the vast country he called Louisiana a possession of his king. All the land that lay along the course of the Mississippi, and all the land traversed by the long river's thousand tributaries, was now French property—a claim to be much disputed but worth fighting for. The new French domain stretched from the Alleghenies in the east to the Rocky Mountains in the west; it held the green forests and blue lakes of the beaver country in the north, the wide grassy plains of the west, and the humid, fertile soil in the south.

La Salle and Tonti, after four calamitous years, at last had gone down to the sea. They now had to return northward to tell of a great deed done. The journey was harder, for they had to paddle against the current. Food ran out, and the countryside and the Indians usually provided only meager, grudging sustenance. Halfway through the trip, La Salle got a fever and had to stop. He sent Tonti ahead, to give news of their success to the colony at Michillimackinac.

La Salle's work was hardly over. He must somehow pay his ever-mounting debts. Now that he knew the Mississippi was navigable to the sea, he would try to open a regular trade route down it and begin to establish forts and trading posts at intervals along the way. As the first post he had to replace the destroyed Crèvecoeur with a new fort on the Illinois.

La Salle and Tonti now built Fort St. Louis upon an acre-wide, nearly unassailable rock that rose 150 feet above the Illinois River. (*Le Rocher,* the French called it; Starved Rock, near Utica, is its name today.) Tonti took long trips to urge various Indian tribes to settle nearby; in numbers, and with French help, they would have protection against a common foe—the Iroquois. Within several years some 20,000 Indians dwelled there, hunting and trapping and fishing, growing corn and squashes, and having their squabbles settled by Tonti.

Since the Iroquois' own fur-trading enterprise was threatened by the new settlement's prosperity, in the spring of 1683 they began to prepare for war. La Salle asked Governor Frontenac for help. But his friend had been recalled to France, and the new governor, La Barre, had joined with La Salle's enemies. In letters to Louis XIV, La Barre mocked all of La Salle's accomplishments, including his Louisiana claim. He ignored the requests for soldiers and ammunition, seized La Salle's emissaries, invited the Iroquois to plunder his holdings, and finally grabbed Fort Frontenac. The news came slowly through the wilderness to La Salle. By autumn he realized that to obtain justice he must go to France.

Once again Tonti was left in charge of La Salle's projects. Although La Barre sent soldiers to take over Fort St. Louis, Tonti stayed on. When the Iroquois attack finally came, he and his men combined with the troops and the friendly Indian settlers to withstand a six-day siege. The frustrated Iroquois departed, convinced that the rock was impregnable.

Meanwhile, in France, La Salle called upon Louis XIV and impressed him with his account of the Mississippi journey. The king was so interested in the explorer's proposal to establish a colony at the mouth of the river, controlling the entrance to the continent's center, that he offered him ships, men, and supplies for this new enterprise. He also took action on La Salle's predicament in New France; writing to La Barre to express displeasure at his mistreatment of his loyal subject La Salle, he ordered both of La Salle's forts restored to his men. Tonti and La Forest, another faithful lieutenant, were given captains' commissions and appointed commandants of Fort St. Louis and Fort Frontenac.

Toward the end of 1685, Tonti heard that La Salle's expedition might not have landed at the Mississippi and that two of his supply ships had been sunk. He realized that even with the best of luck, La Salle's situation would be hazardous, since Spain would try to destroy any French colony planted on the shores of the Gulf of Mexico.

Believing that La Salle would need him in his new colony, Tonti collected a group of Canadians and Indians and in January of 1686 started down the Mississippi again, to meet his leader. Coming to the river's mouth, he found no sign of a colony, even after sending search parties east and west along the ocean for a hundred miles. La Salle obviously had missed the river in his voyage from France. Tonti could do nothing now for him except a symbolic deed. The column that La Salle had planted four years before had been knocked down by floods; Tonti moved it to higher ground. Leaving with an Indian chief a letter for La Salle—"the man who will come up the river"—Tonti despondently set off for the north.

At the Arkansas River, Tonti left some Frenchmen to build a fort and trading post upon his seignory, to be the first link-up with Fort St. Louis on the Illinois. (Tonti is sometimes called the "father of Arkansas" because this was the first European settlement in the state. And for some while the Arkansas River was known as *La Rivière de Tonti*—"Tonti's River.")

After returning to Fort St. Louis, Tonti sped off to Montreal, where he and his Indian allies assisted in a massive French attack upon the unruly Iroquois. When Tonti came back at last to the Illinois, he found La Salle's brother and several other men waiting there for him. Father Jean Cavelier assured Tonti that La Salle had been in good health when last seen. But he told him a dismal tale of La Salle's latest venture. His expedition had landed four hundred miles west of the Mississippi; by the time La Salle recognized his error, it was too late to rectify it. In Matagorda Bay on the coast of Texas the isolated little colony had struggled to build fortifications, find food, fend off hostile Indians, evade the Spaniards, maintain discipline, and periodically send out parties to find the Mississippi—for ascending it to Fort St. Louis and Tonti was their only hope of rescue.

Tonti sent La Salle's brother off to Quebec with his own canoes, supplies, and money, confident that he would arrange at once to have La Salle rescued by sea.

Toward the end of the year, Tonti learned from the men at his Arkansas post that La Salle had been murdered by a small band of conspirators in the party that La Salle himself had been leading toward the Mississippi. Father Cavelier and his companions were spared; they had concealed the news of La Salle's death for fear they would be unable to get funds to return to France. This deception was a terrible affront to the honorable Tonti. With horror he listened to the grim details of his friend's death, after which La Salle was even refused burial. "Such was the end of one of the great men of the age," mourned Tonti, "a man of admirable spirit, and capable of undertaking all sorts of explorations."

La Salle's death rang the first knell of France's defeat in North America. But Tonti had no time to sit and grieve. He suspected that Louis XIV, learning of La Salle's death, would simply abandon the pathetic little colony to whatever grim fate offered. So Tonti now started down the Mississippi again, with five Frenchmen and three Indians, on another humane mission: to bring back La Salle's colonists who, knowing nothing of their leader's death, would daily be expecting rescue. Among the settlers there was Tonti's old traveling companion, Father Zenobe Membre.

They came to the Red River in February of 1689, traveled up

it several hundred miles, then headed southwestward, cross-country, toward the lost colony. Tonti's men finally refused to accompany him farther, and only one Frenchman and one Indian remained. The Frenchman fell into a river with the gunpowder bag. Now lacking ammunition, encountering hostile Indians, and without guides to escort them, Tonti reluctantly gave up his rescue mission to the lost colony still a few hundred miles away.

A spring flood covered the land as Tonti and his two companions started back to the Mississippi. "It would be difficult," he wrote later, "to give an idea of the trouble we had to get out of this miserable country, where it rained night and day." For a hundred and fifty miles they waded, or floundered on flimsy rafts; they pushed through acre after acre of dense, cutting reeds; they made campfires and slept in large trees. "In short," said Tonti afterwards (and he was not given to complaining), "I never suffered so much in my life." During the homeward journey, too, he contracted a fever from which he never fully recovered.

By September, Tonti was back at Fort St. Louis, after nearly a year of fruitless wandering. Actually, had he reached La Salle's colony, he would have found it desolate. Smallpox had decimated the settlers, then Indians had slaughtered or made captives of the weakened survivors; and shortly afterwards the Spaniards arrived—too late to annihilate the place.

France's efforts to colonize the New World were faltering. In the troubled New France, both the English and hostile Indians were attacking many settlements. Frontenac, the only governor able to rule firmly, returned to bolster French power. La Salle's old associate was good to La Salle's friend, Tonti. With the governor's approval and assistance, the Italian commandant expanded and strengthened the military and trading post at Fort St. Louis, which had passed into Tonti's possession, along with a portion of La Salle's dreams. On a smaller scale, Tonti continued his fallen leader's work and did what he could to pay off La Salle's debts and to assure him a respected place in history. In 1691, Tonti moved Fort St. Louis and its Indian settlement to a better site downstream. Near present-day Peoria, it was the first permanent European town in the West.

Henri de Tonti married an Indian woman, but there is no record of any children. When a royal edict forbade fort commanders from fur trading, Tonti left Fort St. Louis in a nephew's care in 1696 and joined his cousin Duluth ("the king of the *coureurs de bois*") in the fur-rich country northwest of Lake Superior, in what is now Minnesota. (Tonti had another relative in America; his brother Alfonso helped Cadillac found Detroit and was an early governor there.)

From time to time he traveled south. In the summer of 1698, he escorted missionaries to his Arkansas post. "He greatly facilitated our passage through many nations," wrote Father St. Cosme to his bishop. The priest saw plainly the Indians' awe of The Man with the Iron Hand: "He had only to be in one's company to prevent any insult from being offered." Yet St. Cosme hoped Tonti could serve France in a more important role: "He is the man who best knows these regions; he has twice gone down to the sea; he has been far inland to the most remote tribes, and is beloved and feared everywhere. If it be desired to have discoveries made in this country, I do not think the task could be confided to a more experienced man than he."

In 1693, Tonti had written a memoir of his adventures in America and sent it to the minister of the French colonies, Count de Pontchartrain. In it he enthusiastically described the potential riches in the Mississippi basin and proposed that France settle the area. Tonti's report, rewritten and expanded, became a popular publication in Europe and stirred up new interest in the Mississippi. The French court realized that another effort to colonize the lower Mississippi would have to be made, to prevent the English or Spanish from capturing the entrance to their Louisiana claim.

Tonti offered to lead an expedition to establish a colony by traveling down the Mississippi—a sure way of avoiding La Salle's error. But his proposal was shelved in favor of another landing by sea, entrusted to the Canadian naval hero, Pierre le Moyne, the Sieur d'Iberville. In March of 1700, Iberville located the Mississippi. Voyaging upstream, he came to a town where Indians gave him the "speaking bark" that Tonti fourteen years before had left for "the man who will come up the river."

The new French colony started by Iberville at first barely managed to survive. Several forts and small settlements were built along the Mississippi delta and on the Gulf of Mexico, but most of the settlers were inexperienced frontiersmen. In 1700, Henri de Tonti arrived at the new colony, bringing in ten canoes fifty able backwoodsmen and a cargo of furs to be shipped to France. Thus Tonti made the first delivery of trade goods by floating boats down the Mississippi. He set to work at once. He could build, plant crops, set traps, cure hides, explore the surrounding terrain and make treaties with its Indian inhabitants. Calm, friendly, tactful but firm, he got other men to work too. Thanks partly to Tonti, the precarious French settlements began to put down roots. He himself must have been glad to be carrying out at last this part of La Salle's design for a French empire in America.

When the *Pelican* anchored at Fort St. Louis de la Mobile

in the summer of 1704, it brought supplies from France, new colonists, and wives for the roving settlers. It also carried yellow fever. By autumn a third of the colony's residents had perished. One of them was the man they could least afford to spare. Henri de Tonti died on September 6, 1704.

For years, the Indians along the Illinois River kept the legend that The Man with the Iron Hand took one final trip up the Mississippi, to be with them when he died. And perhaps Tonti's valiant spirit did wander back over the many lands and rivers and lakes he had traversed. If so, the journey was far—north and south, east and west, the breadth of the United States and half its length: for Tonti had passed through what are now Illinois and Indiana, Michigan and Wisconsin and Minnesota, Arkansas and Texas, Louisiana and Mississippi and Alabama.

Italy was his birthplace; France held his allegiance; but America became his home.

He Talked of Freedom

Philip Mazzei

"Wherever I shall be and under any circumstances I will never relent my efforts toward the welfare of my adopted country."

THE ITALIAN MERCHANT in London in 1767 received an order for two of the ingenious stoves designed by Benjamin Franklin. The request came from the Grand Duke of Tuscany, so Philip Mazzei hurried to fill it. He called upon the popular American, then Pennsylvania's agent in London. Franklin told Mazzei that his stoves were not being made in England. The two men searched the shops together and finally found stoves that could be altered to Franklin's design. The Tuscan ruler got the first genuine Franklin stoves in Europe; the dealer who had provided them started a profitable business by making many more; and Philip Mazzei added Franklin to a long list of notable friends—an association that led him to America.

Filippo Mazzei was born in 1730 near Florence in the Italian state of Tuscany. His father and grandfather were prosperous merchants and landowners. After their deaths,

Filippo's eldest brother became a family tyrant: Filippo's hatred of him doubtless started a perpetual battle against all tyrannies, whether physical or ideological.

Wherever Mazzei went during his lifetime—and he lived long and traveled far—his disposition impelled him to discuss and debate almost everything. To many, Philip Mazzei was a parlor gadfly as he buzzed about at the center of conversation; wherever he lighted he stirred up and even stung the ignorant, the prejudiced, the complacent, the selfish. Mazzei believed that every man had the right to freedom of thought: he wanted to see it fully and capably exercised.

Young Filippo Mazzei studied to be a doctor but was expelled from a Florentine hospital because of a minor infraction. Despite the dismissal, he continued to attend medical lectures. Meanwhile he led a gay life about town—courting the ladies, supporting himself by giving dancing lessons, and constantly discoursing on art and politics and philosophy. After a fierce fight with his brother over their inheritance, he decided to go to South America, to make a fortune and then return to Italy for vengeance. But he got no farther than the seaport town of Leghorn, where the townspeople liked the short, dapper, and affable Filippo and persuaded him to stay. There Filippo practiced medicine among the poor.

In 1753, when an elderly Jewish physician from Smyrna asked him to be his assistant, he went to Turkey, where he stayed for three years, busy as a doctor but equally occupied at social gatherings. Then, wishing to return to Europe, he took a position as ship's doctor on a vessel heading for England—the country he considered most likely to please a philosophical and political liberal.

In London, Mazzei undertook commercial commissions for friends, gave Italian lessons to high-class people, and went to medical lectures. His circle of acquaintances quickly grew. When he realized that the English wanted Italian products but were unable to buy them, he opened up a shop that imported wines, olive oil, cheeses, fruits, silk, and candy. Honoring a promise given to a dying friend named Martin, the kindly Mazzei lodged a widow and her young daughter in his living quarters above the store.

By comparison with the tyrannical and reactionary governments on the Continent, England was politically advanced. Yet Mazzei became disillusioned when he saw that many inequities still existed in the English system. He fervently and vocally advocated complete democracy.

After meeting Benjamin Franklin, Mazzei got to know other Americans in London. For long hours he discussed with them the growing conflict between England and her American colonies—caused by the attempt to impose the Stamp Tax and other indignities upon the colonists, who were not allowed representatives in Parliament.

When Mazzei expressed sympathy for the American cause, his new friends urged him to go to America. At first he declined; but his interest deepened when he was assured that the colonists' government was not just "a poor copy of the English system." Hopeful that the Americans would achieve total independence and eager to take part in the formation of a new and ideal form of government, Mazzei talked now of emigrating. Knowledgeable on almost any subject, he chose horticulture as his special gift to America.

Virginia's agent in London, Thomas Adams, wrote about his friend Mazzei to Thomas Jefferson. That able young lawyer serving as a representative in Virginia's House of Burgesses was almost as interested in improving agriculture as he was in achieving civil liberty. Enthusiastically, Jefferson began planning for Mazzei's coming. Letters sailed across the Atlantic, proposing projects that Mazzei could start on American soil. He would plant the first European wine grapes, introduce olive and citrus trees, and attempt the commercial production of silk. Meanwhile, Mazzei's other friends expressed horror at his decision to leave the "civilized" half of the globe. "I never expected such a resolution from a man of sense, as you are," one wrote.

Several years passed by. Once again in Tuscany, gathering up supplies for his American venture, Mazzei fretted over the continuing exile from "my dear Country, mine by choise, not by chance." His vast agricultural undertaking was pared down from lack of funds and various setbacks, but Mazzei still felt confident. "I have 3 constant Friends that I cannot luse, Honesty, Industry and Courage," he wrote to Thomas Adams.

Finally, all was ready. The diligent Mazzei had assembled special farm equipment, vine cuttings, fruit pits and seedlings and grafts, and seeds and plants of vegetables as yet unknown in America. Leopold, the Grand Duke of Tuscany, had approved of Mazzei's mission and had given him permission to take with him ten vineyard workers, some farmers, and a tailor. Mrs. Martin and her seventeen-year-old daughter, still in Mazzei's care, were going too.

The ship left Leghorn in September of 1773; three months later it docked in Virginia. To pay debts, Mazzei sent the ship back to Italy loaded with grain, flour, and tobacco.

In Williamsburg, the colony's capital, Mazzei was warmly welcomed at the home of Jefferson's brother-in-law. Many of the members of the Assembly came to meet the Italian immigrant, among them the eminent lawyer George Wythe, and George Washington, the wealthy Virginia gentleman who had proven a good military leader in the French and Indian war.

To Mazzei's surprise and pleasure, the Virginia legislature granted him five thousand acres for his agricultural experiments. But when he learned that the acreage consisted of small, separate parcels, he declined the gift. He set off westward with Thomas Adams to look over some land next to Adams' tract. On the way they stopped to visit Jefferson at Monticello.

Through their mutual friend, Jefferson and Mazzei already knew much about each other. Now, at their meeting, Jefferson was charmed by the effervescent Italian, and Mazzei felt much at home with the rangy, red-haired, plain-speaking young American. The two men's interests were inexhaustible. They talked far into the night: of soil and crops; of the American colonies' troubles with England; of religion and political theories; of fine wines and Italian cuisine; of art, architecture, music, literature, and science.

In the early morning Jefferson took Mazzei around his plantation. Gazing at the country around Monticello—fertile, rolling, warmed by the southern sun—Mazzei was reminded of his homeland. Here was what he had hoped to find in America. And now Jefferson was telling him that a farm adjoining his property was up for sale; if Mazzei would buy it, he would contribute several thousand acres of his own land to the enterprise. Gratefully, Mazzei accepted the offer. The land was good; but even better would be the proximity to Jefferson. Mazzei could not possibly have found a more intelligent, civilized, inspiring, and companionable neighbor in all of America. Mazzei decided to call his American homesite *Colle* ("hill" in Italian), in keeping with Monticello ("little mountain").

While Mazzei was returning to Williamsburg to fetch his workers, Thomas Adams began to urge him to marry Mrs. Martin. The reluctant Mazzei feared that the small signs of vanity and pride which he had noticed in her might expand, "were she to pass from a state of dependence to that of mistress of my house." But Adams' insistence finally got the better of his caution: the couple was soon married.

At Williamsburg Mazzei applied for citizenship. He also visited Lord Dunmore, the unpopular governor of Virginia. "As he thought he might make a proselyte of me," Mazzei recorded, "we became so intimate that it was easy for me to see the weakness of his mind and the meanness of his heart." He returned to Monticello and reported to Jefferson what the governor had said. Mazzei was firmly convinced by now that war was inevitable, even though most Americans at the time hoped that compromise might avoid rupture and bloodshed.

Mazzei lived at Monticello during the spring of 1774 while he built his home at Colle; there he and his host constantly discussed the mounting crisis in the American colonies. During the day Mazzei set out vineyards and orchards and planted vegetables, often accompanied by the intrigued Jefferson, who began bestowing Italian names to his own vegetables. Already an Italophile—a lover of things Italian—Jefferson had taught himself the Italian language, but until Mazzei came into his life he had not spoken it. Jefferson also admired Mazzei's workers: their skill, strength, and sheer love for the land. Believing those men best who lived close to the soil, Jefferson proposed that immigration from Italy be encouraged.

Jefferson had not yet crossed the Atlantic, so he was fascinated with Mazzei's comments on life and politics in

Europe. Mazzei had little liking for any of the existing governments and championed the founding in America of a true republic. Feeling that war was well on its way, he knew that it was time for Americans to consider the best type of government they could establish, if they won complete freedom. He insisted that Jefferson and the other American statesmen still had too much respect for the English constitution. They were accustomed "to look upon England as a model of perfection." When he pointed out a number of defects in the English form of government, Jefferson said that many had not occurred to him. Of course not, Mazzei explained. "Ever since childhood you have heard that it was the best possible type of government." And there had not been any compelling reason for Jefferson to examine it in detail.

Leaders in the thirteen colonies corresponded with each other about their mutual problems, then met in 1774 in the First Continental Congress to set a course for the future. Most of them were still trying to steer cautiously between submission to England and a total break with the "mother country." The two men at Monticello wondered how much the ordinary Americans knew; to prepare them for the possibility of war, Jefferson and Mazzei began to write articles which were published in a newsletter. Their propaganda essays outlined the reasons for the conflict with England, urged the establishment of complete political liberty, and suggested the formation of "Independent Companies" of militia—Americans prepared to fight, when and if that proved necessary. Mazzei's articles, signed "Furioso," were translated at first into English by Jefferson, but then the American urged Mazzei to write directly in English, which for a time he corrected but later kept intact. "That phraseology is not pure English," he said, "but everyone will understand you, and the effect will be more forceful. That is what matters."

"To attain our goal it is necessary, my dear citizens, to discuss the natural rights of man and the foundations of a free government," Mazzei told his readers. "All men are by nature equally free and independent. This equality is essential to the establishment of a liberal government. . . . A truly republican form of government cannot exist except where all men—from the very rich to the very poor—are perfectly equal in the natural rights."

Busy as he was with thinking, talking, and writing, Mazzei also worked hard to make a success of Colle. He formed a company to finance and regulate the agricultural enterprise and sold shares to a number of prominent Virginians, among them George Washington, Peyton Randolph, John Page, George Mason, Thomas Adams, Thomas Jefferson, and even Lord Dunmore.

But Mazzei's start at Colle was unlucky. In early May a late frost froze many of his vines and fruit trees from Italy so that the tender young leaves fell and left orchards barren and grape vines stunted for a year. He found some consolation in the luxuriant native vegetation around him, especially the wild grape vines, unaffected by the frost and growing as high as trees. One of his farmers advised him, "Master, don't write home about it, because nobody there would believe you. . . ." In the fall, Mazzei made some wine from these grapes. "This country is better calculated than any other I am acquainted with for the produce of wine," Mazzei wrote to George Washington.

Mazzei was often invited to social gatherings away from Colle, where the principal topic was, of course, the colonies' troubles with England. Mazzei invariably dominated these

conversazioni—as he called them—with his witty and tren-
chant comments on English politics. In the informal meetings
he helped dispose the Virginia leaders toward an open break
with England; he was clearing the way for the irreverent and
forceful arguments coming later in Thomas Paine's inflama-
tory, highly influential tract, *Common Sense.*

Mrs. Mazzei's presence at these social affairs was rarely appreciated. As Mazzei had feared, her small faults grew
gigantic. She was domineering, haughty, greedy—unbearable,
in short. Mazzei avoided her company, for when they were
together they quarreled loudly and incessantly.

The clash between redcoats and Americans at Concord and
Lexington in the spring of 1775 led to rupture with the
mother country. In early July of 1776, Thomas Jefferson, a
member of the Second Continental Congress, wrote the
Declaration of Independence. In it he gave an American immortality to Philip Mazzei when he sharpened his Italian
friend's phrase, "All men are by nature equally free and independent," into five words that would shape the attitude of
the emerging nation and ring down loud and clear through
the years: "All men are created equal." Jefferson sent one of
his few copies of the document to Mazzei; he in turn proudly
sent a copy to the Grand Duke of Tuscany, hoping that the
wealthy ruler would be impressed and someday might prove
helpful to the Americans.

When Lord Dunmore brought British soldiers to Virginia
to raze the coast, the Independent Companies of volunteers,
which Mazzei and Jefferson had urged into existence, roused
to drive him out. With two other Italians, Mazzei set off for
the coast; they marched for days, sleeping in the woods at
night. They met other volunteers, one of them young James
Madison, a future friend of both Mazzei and Jefferson. Close

to their destination, they learned that the British had already been defeated—the news brought to them by Patrick Henry, whose fiery speeches had helped join Americans together in a common cause. As Henry commended the assembled volunteers on their patriotism, Mazzei felt that he looked particularly at the three Italians.

Jefferson, busy at the Congress and then serving in Virginia's new legislature at Williamsburg, could not often return to Monticello. During his absences, Mazzei was regarded as the leader of Albemarle County. From near and far people came to him "for light on the true state of our affairs." As evidence of their confidence in him, he was one of twelve men elected to represent the county's voters, to consult with the legislators at Williamsburg and to instruct the citizens about important proposals. Mazzei worked hard to enlist public support for Jefferson's bill to establish complete religious freedom in Virginia. Each Sunday he spent at a different church, giving speeches to convince its members that no church should be state-preferred and -supported, as the Established Church of England had been.

At some other time in history Mazzei might have happily spent the rest of his life at Colle. But war had come. Mazzei's experimental farm was virtually neglected. "I was more taken up with national affairs than with my own," he said. Most of his farmers either joined the army or were lured away by other landowners, and he could not import new workers because of British inference with shipping.

And Jefferson now gave Mazzei a job. The condition of American finances was deplorable. Knowing that the Duke of Tuscany lent out at interest portions of his great fortune to other countries, Jefferson proposed that the Americans borrow money from Leopold. In letters to John Adams and

John Hancock, Jefferson asked that Congress send someone to broach the subject with Leopold. "I think we have a gentleman here who would do it with dexterity and fidelity," he wrote of Mazzei. When Congress failed to respond, Jefferson arranged instead for Mazzei to represent Virginia: if he could get money or credit from the Tuscan ruler, better it go to one American state than to none.

In the spring of 1779, Mazzei sold most of his belongings and rented Colle to Baron Riedesel, a German general who had been captured with his Hessian troops at Saratoga. In June of 1779, the Mazzeis left Virginia on a ship bound for France. Fearing British seizure, Mazzei had put his official papers into a bag weighted down by lead. When the vessel was captured thirty miles out at sea—prearranged, Mazzei suspected, by the traitorous captain—Mazzei hurled overboard the incriminating evidence of his secret mission. He was taken to New York, where for three months he was kept prisoner. Since no evidence was found of his connection with the rebellious state of Virginia, he and his family were finally allowed to resume their voyage. Sending his termagant wife off to a sister in Calais, Mazzei headed for Paris, there to lay the groundwork for his financial negotiations in Europe and to await the arrival of duplicates of his Virginia commission and instructions, necessary for transacting any business.

In Paris in early 1790, Mazzei made himself at home immediately among the French liberals and intellectuals. He struck up an acquaintance with the Marquis de la Fayette, back for a time from his service with General Washington. And he sought out his old friend Benjamin Franklin, the American Minister Plenipotentiary, who was enlisting French support for the struggling American nation. Franklin disapproved of Mazzei's mission; he felt that borrowing from abroad should be handled only by the national government.

Mazzei busied himself on America's behalf in a hundred ways. He talked with influential people and imbued them with confidence in the solidity and future prosperity of the new country. He wrote newspaper articles to defend the War for Independence and to extol the first beginnings of a republican government. He sent frequent reports to Jefferson, now governor of Virginia, informing him of European attitudes and events. He contrived a plan whereby the American land forces and French navy together could "bottle up" the British in New York, and communicated it to French officers (who later put the strategem to use at Yorktown and forced Cornwallis's surrender, bringing the war to an end). With delight, Mazzei studied the effect on the Continent of the American fight for freedom. "The Notions of Equality among mankind have made of late a most rapid and Surprising progress in Europe," he wrote Jefferson. "All judicious and Sensible people agree that this happy and noble improvement is chiefly owing to our Glorious cause, by the noise of which the minds of the people have been shakened and awakened."

Asking Franklin to forward his mail to him, Mazzei went on to Italy in June of 1780. He was especially anxious to receive his commission, which, despite his pleas to Jefferson, had not arrived. In Florence, Mazzei called upon the Grand Duke and told him much about America. By autumn he still had not received the official papers, and reproached Jefferson (who was having his own great troubles in office): "To be deprived of the power of being of real service at this time is cruel, and my state of uncertainty gives me more uneasiness than I can express." Mazzei suspected that Franklin was not sending on his mail from Paris.

Mazzei tried to keep up a good appearance. He wrote long

articles for Italian newspapers and composed letters to Leopold, all on the subject of the new American nation. But it was useless. The Tuscan duke would not part with a single *scuda*. Also, since Franklin's success in getting French assistance was now turning the war in the Americans' favor, Mazzei found little use for the duplicate papers from Jefferson, when they arrived eighteen months late.

Mazzei left Italy for the north. He stayed for a few days with his stepdaughter, who had married an impecunious young count named Etienne de Rieux, and he offered to find a place for the newlyweds in America. There the Revolutionary War was ended; the truce with England had just been signed in Paris. Mazzei now took a ship homeward—to the United States of America, which he by his eager and tireless efforts as an "assistant Founding Father" had helped to create.

When he arrived in Virginia in November of 1783, Mazzei met with disappointment. His experimental farm at Colle had been devastated during the war years. The whole project would have to be started anew. Now in his mid-fifties, Mazzei could not muster the strength for the job—especially since his neighbor at Monticello would not be there to encourage him. Jefferson was going to Paris to replace Franklin. Away at the Congress in Annapolis, he wrote to offer Mazzei the hospitality of Monticello. But the near-deserted mansion depressed Mazzei; Jefferson's wife had died there the year before.

Mazzei took stock of himself. His attachment to America had become a thing of spirit, not of soil. His zeal now, as he later described it to Jefferson, was "not for the trees or the rivers or for the land of America but for the asylum of liberty." Promoting that ideal of freedom was what he wished to do in the years remaining to him.

Mazzei finally settled his account with the state of Virginia, which owed him for four years' service as an agent in Europe. Governor Benjamin Harrison, when paying him, commended him on his "patriotic exertions." To complicate Mazzei's life, his stepdaughter and her husband arrived prematurely in America. He paid for their passage, then lent them Colle. He himself went to live in Richmond, the new state capital, and there he gladly resumed the *conversazioni* on political topics. Alas, Mrs. Mazzei—"that malicious viper"—reappeared, pursuing her daughter and intent upon making her husband's life miserable. She started a Bill of Chancery against him and attempted to seize his property. Since divorce was not yet possible in America, Mazzei decided that he could escape his wife only by returning to Europe.

Mazzei wanted to serve his adopted country as a consul in some European court; he prepared to go to Annapolis to seek an appointment from Congress. "I tremble at the idea," wrote the alarmed Jefferson to James Madison. "I know that he will be worse to me than a return of my double quotidian headach." Knowing well the volume of talk and drama that always accompanied the voluble Tuscan, Jefferson feared that at Annapolis, where the new nation's leaders were trying to establish an orderly government, Mazzei's presence might touch off a feud that could split the whole convocation apart. To stop Mazzei from coming, Jefferson told Madison to inform him that Congress had already decided to make native American birth a requisite for consulship.

Mazzei was cast adrift. Now he would be unable even to serve America abroad. Yet he must escape his wife; and creditors were plaguing him. By turns a doctor, merchant, horticulturist, pamphleteer, and financial agent, he could not find another proper role. Realizing that Jefferson was departing for Paris without having seen him or given advice, Mazzei suffered a "terrible blow." He wrote forlornly to him: "I find myself in a labyrinth; and my mind, tired and weakened, wanders in incertitude."

Mazzei left America in June of 1785. He had entrusted James Madison with settling his business affairs, and now he wrote to him: "I am leaving but my heart remains. America is my Jupiter, Virginia my Venus. . . . I know well that wherever I shall be and under any circumstances I will never relent my efforts toward the welfare of my adopted country."

In Paris, Mazzei at once sought out Thomas Jefferson and introduced the new Minister Plenipotentiary to all his illustrious friends. He continuously praised the United States to everyone; and to refute the errors and unjust criticisims in a book recently published about the new American nation, Mazzei undertook a project that ran into four volumes when published in 1788: *Studies of the Historical and Political Origins of the United States of North America,* by "A Citizen of Virginia." It was the first accurate history of the new nation. But Mazzei's hopes of earning money from it came to naught. Frenchmen, embroiled in their own revolution, found little time for reading.

Mazzei had been in America during the first years of the War for Independence; now he was in France during the early, turbulent years of the French Revolution. And although he and Jefferson, with the other founding member of the "Club of 1789," urged moderation, their sane voices were scarcely heard in the country's mounting chaos.

As usual, Mazzei lacked funds. James Madison did his best to collect money owed to Mazzei in America; it took years for Mazzei to be repaid. As he and Madison exchanged frequent letters over this and other business, Mazzei often gave Madison—at work on constructing the Constitution of the United States—his opinions on government past, present, and future. "It is of infinite importance to the cause of liberty to ascertain the degree of it which will consist with the purposes of society," he advised. "An error on one side may be as fatal as on the other." This he knew from observing France.

Mazzei corresponded too with John Adams, then the American minister in London. Adams was disturbed over the "shameless falsehoods" told about the United States throughout Europe. "The real motive is to discourage Emigration," Adams told Mazzei. Germans, English, Scots, Irish, French . . . all would "fly to America for relief from that intolerable Load which they now carry on their shoulders, if they knew the true state of facts in America. . . ."

In 1788, Mrs. Mazzei had died at Colle; she was buried in Monticello's graveyard. Jefferson commented that her death returned to Mazzei "three-quarters of the globe elbow-room, which he had ceded to her, on condition she would leave him quiet in the fourth." Although anxious to return to America, Mazzei had become a private intelligencer in Paris for the King of Poland. He faithfully served the liberal Stanislaus II, and in 1791 was called to Poland to be an adviser. When that hapless country was split among Russia, Austria, and Germany in the following year, Mazzei left for Italy and settled in Pisa.

Jefferson had returned to America, to become the Secretary of State in President Washington's first cabinet. Inspecting Colle, he reported its deterioration to Mazzei: "All the houses at Colle are become mere ruins, except the dwelling house." The orchards had long since disappeared. Mazzei asked Jefferson to sell the property for him. Jefferson did and then reinvested Mazzei's money; financial business went on between them for years.

In 1795, Mazzei received a letter from Jefferson which told of the conflict between the Federalists, headed by John Adams and Alexander Hamilton, and the Anti-Federalists or Republicans, of whom Jefferson had become spiritual leader, assisted by James Madison. "The aspect of our politics has wonderfully changed since you left us," Jefferson wrote. "In place of that noble love of liberty and republican government which carried us triumphantly thro' the war, an Anglican, monarchical and aristocratical party has sprung up, whose avowed object is to draw over us the substance as they have already done the forms of the British government. . . . It would give you a fever were I to name to you the apostates who have gone over to these heresies, men who were Samsons in the field and Solomons in the council. . . . In short we are likely to preserve the liberty we have obtained only by unremitting labors and perils. But we shall preserve them. . . ."

Jefferson had written rashly, in angry concern, to his Italian friend, never suspecting that the letter would be read by others; he had written hyperbolically too, since he knew the Tuscan appreciated colorful drama. Mazzei always liked to reveal interesting news from the United States, so he translated the letter and gave it to an Italian newspaper. The French took it up; then the English translated it from the French—both interpreting it as evidence of American hostility and political upheaval. When Jefferson's words, in a different English than he had written, reached American shores in the spring of 1797, a political tempest already in the brewing broke upon his head. The infamous "Mazzei Letter" discredited Jefferson for some time with many of his countrymen; there were insults in it for almost everyone. Jefferson's relations with Washington had been going badly; now they were severed, and Washington never spoke to him again. The letter might have exiled Jefferson forever from national affairs, but between the time of writing it and its appearance in America he had become Vice President under John Adams.

Jefferson's correspondence with Mazzei continued, but thereafter went more cautiously. Mazzei frequently filled Jefferson's requests for books and wines. He sent him seeds and pits, and even plants, which often failed to survive the long Atlantic crossing or did not prosper when planted at Monticello. Mazzei in turn requested seeds and grafts from his famous American friend, who even in the busiest days of his presidency took time out to chat with Mazzei about a variety of matters.

In 1796, Philip Mazzei had married a woman younger by fifty years. Two years later his only child, Elisabetta, was born. ("This child is now my diversion," wrote the fond old father to Jefferson, "and my occupations are almost entirely divided between her and the garden.") In 1802, still owed a salary from the deposed Polish king and concerned about supporting his family, Mazzei journeyed all the way to St. Petersburg to ask for payment. The Russian emperor, impressed with Mazzei's determined quest, offered him the choice of a lump sum or an annual pension. Mazzei chose the latter; he was in good health and expected to remain so for a long time.

In 1805, Benjamin Latrobe, the designer of the new American capital at Washington, D.C., asked for Mazzei's help in finding a good Italian sculptor to work on the new public buildings there. In his letter Latrobe graciously added: "The time is already approaching when our vines and our olives will spread your name and our gratitude over a great portion of the country."

The elderly Mazzei undertook this new assignment with characteristic energy and enthusiasm. And he wrote to Jefferson: "I thank you for it with all my heart, for I know that it is through you that I have the honor and privilege of being placed in a position to do something for my dear adopted fatherland." He soon located two talented young sculptors willing to emigrate.

For years Mazzei wished for some consular job in Italy, serving the United States; his hopes were always disappointed. In this exile, however, he helped the new nation in many local matters. He really longed to take his wife and daughter to America, away from the confusion of the Napoleonic wars, far from the despotic governments of the Italian states. But he would have no way of supporting them in America—and there no Colle belonged to him now to provide a roof over their heads.

The years passed by. Meanwhile, Mazzei tended his garden, watched his little girl grow up, and corresponded with his many friends in other lands. In 1813, he finished his memoirs, written as a long letter to a friend. (They were not published until 1845.) Mazzei hoped that Jefferson would visit Italy, and then take him back with him to America, where he wished to be buried. But his old friend never came; and Mazzei did not see again his adopted country, to whom he gave his love and loyalty and where he had counted among his friends the first four presidents.

Mazzei's friend Jefferson, in summing him up, said: "He

had some peculiarities, but who of us has not? But he was of solid worth; honest, able, zealous in sound principles, moral and political, constant in friendship, and punctual in all his undertakings."

Philip Mazzei died at Pisa in 1816, at the age of eighty-five. He left to the generations after him in America the planting of grape vines and the passionate *conversazioni* far into the night on the subject of freedom.

The Artist of the Capitol

Constantino Brumidi

"My one ambition and my daily prayer is to make
beautiful the Capitol of the one country on earth
where there is liberty."

Every year a million people touring the Capitol in Washington, D.C., see murals that an Italian artist painted a century ago. Several thousand visitors a day walk up the steps
leading to the great circular rotunda beneath the dome which
symbolizes the United States government and crowns the
massive structure where our national legislatures sit: the Senate in the south, the House of Representatives in the north.

Entering the rotunda, the guests are greeted by renowned
Americans of the past—bronze and marble statues lining the
walls, on which are large oil paintings of scenes from American history. Gazing upwards some fifty feet, spectators see a
fresco frieze girdling the round room; painted in muted
grays to imitate sculpture, it shows landmarks in the settlement of the New World. Then straight above, at the very
"eye" of the dome 180 feet above the floor, is the Capitol's
largest painting: the famous fresco of the "Apotheosis of

Washington," the glorification of the "Father of Our Country."

Both the frieze and the vast dome fresco were painted by Constantino Brumidi, an Italian immigrant who devoted the last part of his life, more than a quarter of a century, to bringing the traditional mural art of his homeland to the walls of the Capitol. After his arrival in America, he was offered many commissions when his talent and experience became known; most of them he declined. "I have no longer any desire for fame or fortune," he explained. "My one ambition and my daily prayer is to make beautiful the Capitol of the one country on earth where there is liberty."

Constantino Brumidi was born in Rome on July 26, 1805. His mother was Italian, his father a Greek who had fled Turkish oppression. As a boy he showed an exceptional talent for drawing and was sent to the Academy of Fine Arts in Rome. At the age of thirteen he entered the famed Academia di San Lucca, where he studied painting and sculpture with master craftsmen. When his apprenticeship was over, Brumidi was given regular work at the Vatican by Gregory XVI as the art-loving Pope built, rebuilt, decorated, and redecorated, all for the splendor of the Church. Brumidi was also employed by a wealthy banker named Prince Alessandro Torlonia to do frescoes and sculptures for his palazzo (later to be Mussolini's residence in Rome).

Pius IX, becoming Pope in 1846, continued the Vatican's paramount claims on Brumidi's artistry. Brumidi helped to restore the deteriorated Raphael frescoes in the loggia; he painted two portraits of the Pope; he assisted in depicting the "Chronology of the Popes" in the new basilica of St. Paul. As a sign of favor, Brumidi was made Captain of the Papal Guards—a position of responsibility in those troubled times.

Pope Pius IX at first had been hailed as a champion of liberty. He granted a constitution to the people of Rome and the surrounding Papal States, but pressures from his cabinet and from reactionary rulers elsewhere caused him to rescind it. Angry and disgusted, the Romans began the Revolution of 1848. The Pope fled to Naples, and the Roman citizens established an orderly republican government.

During the insurrection Brumidi refused the command to fire upon his own people—an act of disobedience that blacklisted him with the Church officials. Like other Romans, Brumidi was moved by the sight of the patriot leader Garibaldi, riding through the streets in his famous red shirt, surrounded by ragged but fiercely loyal soldiers. The artist, in his early forties, became a revolutionary too.

Liberty reigned but briefly in Rome. After the exiled Pope appealed to all the Catholic powers to help restore him, Louis Napoleon of France sent his army toward Rome, to occupy it before the rival Austrians arrived. French soldiers attacked the city and finally forced its surrender. Garibaldi escaped, to begin an exile of almost ten years (one of them spent in America on Staten Island, where he worked in a candle factory). Brumidi, remaining in Rome, was sentenced to prison, but his release was arranged after fourteen months by the Pope himself, on the condition that he leave Rome forever. Before he went, however, he finished some work he had undertaken before the revolution.

Constantino Brumidi came to New York in September of 1852. There he painted portraits of several prominent families; his first important commission was to paint a huge altarpiece in St. Stephen's Church. In November, he formally declared his intention to become a naturalized American citizen and took out his first papers. He then went to Mexico to paint a mural in the Cathedral of Mexico City. On his return, he began the work that would occupy the rest of his life: the decoration of the Capitol.

Italian artists were no strangers to Washington, D.C. The first two sculptors to work there, Giovanni Andrei and Giuseppe Franzoni, had been sent over by Philip Mazzei to embellish the new city's public buildings. Through the years a succession of sculptors from Italy had carved statues, bas-reliefs, and ornate capitals for columns. Italy was judged the natural home for sculptors; all the Americans who did sculpture work for the capital had at least studied there. As yet, however, no Italian painter had been employed in Washington.

Captain Montgomery Meigs, an Army engineer who supervised new constructions for the Capitol, was looking for a muralist, especially one skilled in the technique of true fresco, which incorporates paintings into the architecture itself. Few Americans had ever attempted murals in public buildings; none had ever used *buono fresco*. Painting in America had developed slowly because of the Puritan prohibition on decoration. Now Americans were primarily easel painters. Using water colors and oils, they earned their livings by painting still lifes, pleasant landscapes, or commissioned portraits.

Mural art, however, was quite different from pictures on canvas. Murals had to stay put. They were painted "for the ages"—or for as long as a building stood. A wall painting in a public building would have to be seen, enjoyed, and understood by a multitude of people through the years. Only Italians were schooled in the *buono fresco* technique, for it was an important art tradition in which they took great pride. Thus, when Captain Meigs searched for a fresco painter, he had to get an Italian. He heard about Constantino Brumidi, and a meeting was arranged.

In 1854, the Capitol's two large extensions, or annexes, were nearly finished. The oldest part of the building, which had suffered many mishaps (such as being burned by the British in 1814), occupied the central part of the enormous structure designed by Thomas U. Walter, the Architect of the Capitol. As the new marble extensions were added, they dwarfed the old copper-covered wooden dome at the center; it would have to be replaced by a much larger dome. This new dome, fashioned after St. Peter's in Rome and to rise more than 300 feet, was just being started when Brumidi toured the Capitol.

Brumidi viewed with an Italian muralist's eyes the long stark hallways, the white, spartan meeting and reception rooms; inevitably, he contrasted them with the colorful paintings adorning the revered buildings in his homeland. For an energetic and idealistic artist the Capitol provided acres of white walls that invited brush, colors, and patriotic subjects. To Brumidi it seemed a natural and worthy place to bring the twenty-centuries-old tradition of Italian fresco art. Just as the European churches for centuries had glorified Christianity, at the Capitol he could substantiate the very spirit of American freedom and portray the men who had won it.

Captain Meigs hired Brumidi and gave him his first commission: the decoration of the Agriculture Committee Room in the House of Representatives, which was to offer the "first example of real fresco in America."

Brumidi set to work in the customary way. First he made his "working sketch," an oil painting on canvas that showed the overall design for a mural. Then he drew "cartoons" on large sheets of stiff paper—outlines of the figures in the size they would assume in the mural itself. When he was ready to begin the fresco, Brumidi engaged several helpers. A workman applied fresh plaster to the wall area to be painted during one day. Meanwhile, Brumidi was preparing his paints by mixing dry tempera with water. An assistant artist would "pounce" the figure outlines onto the fresh plaster by dusting powdered charcoal through perforations in the cartoons or by etching lines on the wet surface by going over the drawings with a stylus. Then Brumidi began painting by brushing his colors upon the plaster; he first did underpainting and flat surfaces, then worked on details and the modeling of light and shadow. Sometimes his assistant would paint in the backgrounds. At the close of the day's work, a workman removed any unpainted plaster before it dried. On the following work day the whole process was repeated in an adjoining area of the fresco. During the long drying period, the lime in the plaster combined with carbon dioxide to make a surface that looked like marble and was almost as durable. The paint lightened and seemed crystalline.

Brumidi's decoration of the Agriculture Committee Room was completed in 1855. On the walls he had frescoed two scenes: "Cincinnatus Summoned from the Plow to Become the Dictator of Rome" and an American subject as its companion, "Putnam Summoned from the Plow to Fight for Independence." He also did two mural paintings in oil: the cutting of grain with a sickle, and the modern-day harvesting of grain with a McCormick reaper. On the ceiling were frescoes with scenes of the four seasons.

Brumidi went on to design the ornate bronze railings that run down the four staircases leading from the House and Senate chambers. On them cherubs, eagles, and deer frolic among corn and wheat. Even today these are known as the "Brumidi Stairways."

In the Senate extension Brumidi took five years to decorate the President's Room—the most opulent of all the rooms in the Capitol, and considered by many art experts to be Brumidi's best work. The room was intended for the use of the President whenever he visited the Capitol. (Today it is usually used for important senators' press conferences.) In the prosperous years before the Civil War, no expense seemed too great to lavish upon the sumptuous room; its gold-plated chandelier alone cost $25,000. Gold-edged mirrors reflected the Brumidi decorations: elegant panels containing portraits of Washington and the five members of his first cabinet, all within rococo "frames" actually painted upon the wall. At the ceiling's four vaulted corners Brumidi portrayed men representing forces in the civilization of America: his countrymen Columbus and Vespucci for discovery and exploration; William Brewster for religion; and Benjamin Franklin for history.

During the late 1850s, Brumidi painted a large mural in the House of Representatives chamber. He proudly signed the painting of Cornwallis surrendering to Washington at Yorktown: "C. Brumidi, citizen of the United States." Granted citizenship in 1857, he may have wanted to display it in front of Congressmen belonging to the anti-foreigner Know-Nothing Party, who believed that America should belong only to native Americans.

Citizen though he was, Brumidi often felt unwelcome. Meigs' choice of him as the artist to decorate the Capitol had not pleased American-born artists who desired regular employment and the chance to display their own talents upon the Capitol's walls. Most of them had no understanding of fresco technique; none had training or experience in it, and an adequate apprenticeship would take years. And had they known the difficulties of the work itself, few if any artists would have wanted to try it.

Fresco painting imposed many limitations. An artist must work quickly, as the plaster dried quickly; he must work skillfully too, as changes and erasures were difficult; his palette or choice of colors was narrow, confined to pigments that would safely combine with lime. Only through years of experience, through trial and error, did the artist really learn to do competent frescoes. Then there was the matter of the muralist's physical problems. Most of the time he stood upon high and unsteady scaffolding; or if he were painting a ceiling, he lay flat on his back, while the paint he applied spattered down upon his face. And meanwhile he was often subjected to the commentary of interested but often ill-informed bystanders, as well as the noise, distractions, and drafts in any public building. It was hardly preferable to the privacy and relative comfort of an artist painting in his own studio.

But Brumidi's critics had simply decided that Brumidi was a bad artist. One, who signed himself "Officious," wrote to Captain Meigs: "I take leave to say that the wall painting, 'The Surrender of Cornwallis,' is execrable, in view of all of which I suggest to you to have the painting wiped out." And if Meigs did not, a conspiracy would oust him from office. . . .

Brumidi's subject matter made another source for complaint. A Congressman harangued about the Agriculture Committee Room frescoes: "Overhead we have pictures of Bacchus, Ceres, and so on, surrounded with cupids, cherubs, etc., to the end of heathen mythology. All this we have; but not a single specimen of the valuable breeds of cattle, horses, sheep, etc., which are now found in this country. . . . But worst of all, there is not a single picture to represent maize." (Yet a fellow Representative was maintaining, "What, sir, can be more beautiful than the fresco work in the room of the Agriculture Committee?")

The disputes over Brumidi's work became public. In 1858, a petition of grievance, "Memorial of the Artists of the United States," was presented to Congress with the signatures of 127 artists. They proposed that artists from their own group be elected to an Art Commission, "who shall be channels for the distribution of all appropriations to be made by Congress for art purposes." Obviously, they did not want Brumidi on the payroll.

The petition was studied by a House committee, whose five members found merit in it. Their own conclusions further denigrated Brumidi's artistry: "A plain coat or two of whitewash is better, in the opinion of this committee, for a temporary finish than the tawdry and exuberant ornamentation with which many of the rooms and passages are being crowded." Furthermore, the committee had been made "painfully conscious that the work has been prosecuted by foreign workmen under the immediate supervision of a foreigner." As a consequence, the Committee found "nothing in the design and execution of the ornamental work of the Capitol, thus far, which represents our own country, or the genius and taste of her artists."

Washington and New York newspapers covered the dispute; some wrote editorials adding to the attack upon Brumidi. Guglielmo Gajani loyally defended his friend Brumidi in the New York *Daily Tribune*. Throughout Europe, he pointed out, public buildings were decorated with the same style, symbols, and classical allegories used by

Brumidi. "Before condemning him," said Gajani, "you must find fault with all the best painters who preceded him, and especially with Michelangelo and Raphael who introduced that style of fresco in the Vatican itself." Gajani mentioned that Brumidi's work at the Vatican and in the Torlonia palazzo was much praised by visitors from abroad. "Should an American admire the works of Brumidi at home," he reasoned, "and despise them when he finds them at Washington?"

Constantino Brumidi also had defenders in Congress. A Representative from Pennsylvania said he was surprised that no one had spoken up "to do justice to those who have devoted their lives and energies to the embellishment of our public buildings." The artist himself must have felt puzzled by the disturbance he was unintentionally causing. As the "Artist of the Capitol" he worked diligently, painting inspirational subjects as best he knew how. A serious student of the classics in literature, philosophy, and history, Brumidi did long research and thought deeply about each painting he undertook. True, he was foreign-born; but he was now an American citizen—and a more proud or loyal citizen could not have been found among the native-born Americans.

The noisy debates over Brumidi's work were silenced when the Civil War came. At first, most work on the Capitol ceased while the city prepared defenses from attacks by the Confederate forces across the Potomac. The heavy marble pillars for the extensions and blocks for the exterior stairs lay scattered about the grounds like fallen soldiers. Newly recruited troops swarmed into the capital, and regiments were quartered in the Capitol building itself. Some soldiers slept in the rotunda, whose new dome was only half-completed; others were bedded down throughout the large building.

Cooking odors filled the corridors, since basement furnaces were used for baking bread and beans for the Union Army.

During those early days of the war Constantino Brumidi doubtless ascended the steep iron stairs (365 in all, like the year's days) that wound around the inside of the Capitol's dome. Coming to the outside balcony, he would have looked out upon a vastly altered city. Washington, D.C. had become an armed camp preparing to defend the nation's founding precepts of equality and liberty for all men. The capital lay at the very border of the split between North and South. Watching his city, Brumidi must have felt almost torn in two, like his adopted country. Jefferson Davis had been a good friend to him. His keen interest in the beautification of the Capitol, first as Senator and then as Secretary of War, had encouraged the Italian artist, especially during the trying years of criticism. Davis had seen to it that Brumidi was given a regular and substantial salary. Other Southerners, too, in Washington had been Brumidi's companions and admirers.

Brumidi had to leave Rome because he had fought in vain for liberty. He came to America expecting to find liberty firmly entrenched there. Serving its cause, with paint and brush, he had spent over five years portraying the achievements and spirit of the American republic upon the Capitol's walls. In wartime Washington Brumidi would stay, hoping to continue to praise in his paintings the essential ideals of America and depict its heroes.

President Lincoln was asked whether work on the Capitol's dome would proceed during wartime. Yes, came his reply. "If the world sees this Capitol going on," Lincoln said, "they will know that we intend the Union shall go on." The President realized that the mighty dome would be the symbol of the American nation to future generations throughout the world.

The 300-foot-high Capitol dome was an engineering masterpiece consisting of two shells, one on top of the other, and weighing nine million pounds. Its completion was officially celebrated on December 2, 1863, by placing a seven-ton statue of the Goddess of Freedom upon the topmost "lantern" (whose thirteen columns symbolized the Union's original states). Following the ceremonial hoisting, guns in the field battery on Capitol Hill saluted and were echoed by artillery in nearby camps. Lincoln's clear intention to preserve the Union was displayed for the world to see.

Now the inside of the dome would be decorated. The new Architect of the Capitol, Edward Clark, considered Brumidi the best artist to paint a gigantic mural on the circular "canopy"—the plaster-covered copper sheet that covered the inside of the dome at its "eye," above the windows that let light into the rotunda. It was a curved surface sixty-five feet in diameter, with a concavity of twenty-one feet. A price of $40,000 was agreed upon, and Brumidi started to work, first doing a detailed working sketch of the subject he chose: "The Apotheosis of Washington."

It was a noble vision—of the stately Washington seated among celestial clouds, with Freedom and Victory as his female companions. The trio was surrounded by thirteen pastel-garbed maidens, each representing one of the original states, who held aloft a banner with the legend *E Pluribus Unum*. Arrayed around these celebrants were six distinct groups of Americans (some of them famous) and Roman gods and goddesses who ruled or inspired particular areas of human endeavor. Armed Liberty, with a shield and a sword, was also there, driving out rebellion and oppression.

Brumidi used his own wife as the model for Freedom. In the early 1860s, the artist had married an attractive young woman named Lola Germon. (He had been married twice before, in Italy.) Her likeness appears frequently among Brumidi's female figures. Then at the height of his fame and earning ability, Brumidi bought a home on G Street. The couple took part in the city's busy social life, and Lola was known as an intelligent conversationalist as well as a great beauty. Very little is known about the marriage, which ended in divorce sometime in the 1870s. A son, Laurence, later unsuccessfully pursued an artistic career.

Starting in early 1865, Brumidi worked almost daily at the dome canopy. He was raised by pulleys to a scaffold he himself designed, and there he sat or lay, painting, for hours at a time, 180 feet above the rotunda floor. In eleven months Brumidi frescoed a phenomenal 4,664 square feet. The design was complicated; painting on a concave surface, Brumidi had to exaggerate many of the figures, to give them normal proportions when viewed from different angles far below.

Brumidi was working on the fresco when the South surrendered. Five days later the President was assassinated. On the 21st and 22nd of April in 1865 some 25,000 people filed into the rotunda to pay their last respects to Lincoln, who lay in state on a black-draped bier beneath Brumidi's unfinished mural in the eye of the dome.

At the end of the year Brumidi put final touches on the gigantic fresco, and the scaffold was removed. The painting was lighted and made ready for public display in January of 1866. Brumidi's most important commission for the Capitol had been finished. For as long as the Capitol stands as the symbol of the American republic, so too will Constantino Brumidi's vision of the enshrinement of Washington.

Yet Brumidi's portrayal of Washington's ultimate glory did not always inspire its beholders with a shared sense of spiritual awe. In his waggish account of his Capitol tour in 1874, Mark Twain spared nobody—architect, sculptor, or painter. Brumidi was no exception. Twain consoled people who were disappointed that visitors no longer were permitted to take the stairway winding inside the dome. "It would be utterly impossible to go up there," Twain cautioned, "without seeing the frescoes in it—and why should you be interested in the delirium tremens of art?" There was some truth in his remark. As one got close to the frescoed figures, they looked like nightmares, with distorted shapes fifteen feet long, painted in rough textures and garish colors. Yet Brumidi had known how to achieve the proper effects: to a viewer on the rotunda floor a ghastly figure above became a lovely damsel in a softly billowing pastel gown.

After the war, Brumidi went on to less monumental tasks. The Capitol still had many blank walls needing embellishments. Brumidi often made suggestions for new work, and to help economize he dropped his regular salary and agreed to work on a *per diem* basis. Congressional appropriations for the art work, however, came sporadically and grudgingly. Sometimes it took several years for the artist to get funds to complete projects already begun.

During the decade after the Civil War, Brumidi worked mainly in the Senate extension. Many of his paintings are in rooms used only by Senators and cannot be seen by the public. He frescoed five large scenes from the Revolutionary War in the South Room (now occupied by the Senate Appropriations Committee); on the ceiling he depicted war emblems and weapons surrounding the head of Liberty. In the North Room, for the Naval Affairs Committee, he painted a ceiling fresco and nine panels with naval themes. In the Senate Reception Room he frescoed the walls and ceiling; in oils he portrayed Washington consulting with Hamilton and Jefferson. He decorated the two rooms used by the Senate District of Columbia Committee—in the smaller room he portrayed allegorically the war between North and South; on the ceiling he showed "Columbia Welcoming the South Back into the Union."

Brumidi covered the walls of the Senate corridors with a profusion of fresco and oil paintings that displayed amazing versatility and keen observation. There were medallions or profiles of renowned Americans; landscapes; studies of children, animals, and birds; shields and zodiac signs; large dramatic scenes from history; and portraits in imitation sculpture, or chiaroscuro. He also supervised the work of assistant artists.

Apart from his continuous decoration of the Capitol, Brumidi occasionally accepted other work, such as the painting of altarpieces in churches in Philadelphia and Washington, murals in private homes, and portrait commissions.

Inevitably, not all Brumidi's prodigious efforts are good art. A sizeable proportion of them are beautiful by traditional, classical standards; many are accurate portrayals; but some, judging with a modern vision, are sentimental or ornate, dull or poor likenesses. Yet in all of Brumidi's works, one can recognize his obvious dedication to beautifying the Capitol. No other artist in America has painted so many actual miles of decorations. In later years Brumidi's paintings were better appreciated by artists who were not personally resentful of his employment and who understood the problems in working with fresco. "I willingly state that this is the best example of fresco painting I have found in the United States," an art critic declared. At the turn of the century an artist decorating the new Congressional Library came to study Brumidi's frescoes. "There is no one who can do such work today," he commented.

In the mid-1870s Brumidi undertook to paint in chiaroscuro—light and shade—the nine-foot-wide panel that circles the rotunda walls fifty-eight feet above the floor. He visualized the 300-foot-long frieze as a "roll of history" recording fifteen significant events in America since Columbus's discovery.

Brumidi was in his early seventies when he began the work. Beset by severe attacks of asthma and rheumatism, the old artist often found his job discomforting. But he needed regular work—and a feeling of usefulness. The pinnacle of his fame and fortune had passed; his young wife had left him; their son was almost a grown man.

From time to time Brumidi, "The Artist of the Capitol," submitted petitions to the government, hoping to be reinstated in a regular salary, so that if feeling poorly or the weather was bad, he could remain at home to work on his designs. The security of a salary was denied him. Yet almost daily, ever dauntlessly, the old man put on his black cape, tucked his long white hair beneath his beret, and reported for work at the Capitol. He was hoisted up in a cage to his "shop"—the scaffold which slid alongside the frieze, suspended from the balcony above. There Brumidi painted from ten till three. His descent was the main attraction of the afternoon at the Capitol. People gathered in the rotunda anxiously and curiously to watch the old artist with the long white beard being slowly lowered to the floor.

In October of 1879, as Brumidi was working on the eighth section of the frieze, his chair on the scaffold tipped backwards and fell. He tumbled too, but somehow managed to catch hold of a ladder rung and cling to life. Brumidi had devoted many years of his life to the Capitol; now it seemed as though the Capitol claimed even his death, in a final ironic sacrifice. But a watchman on a balcony, who had seen the accident and called for help, managed with two other men to pull the artist to safety.

Although Brumidi seemed physically unharmed, the shock proved too disturbing. He did not return to work. Visitors to the Capitol who noticed the unfinished work were told that the old artist would probably never finish his paintings.

At home, Brumidi was trying to complete his frieze designs, so that a younger artist might execute them for him. But his fervent desire failed to sustain him. As his health rapidly declined, Brumidi finally took to his bed. There in his studio he lay, surrounded by his sculptures and some unfinished oil portraits on easels; on the walls were pinned the heavy sheets of paper with the frieze cartoons, to remind him of mankind's aspirations—and human frailties.

When Constantino Brumidi died on February 19, 1880, the Capitol lost a long-familiar figure. "It was the dream of his life that he should come back," wrote the Washington *Post*. "He wanted with his own hand to lead that historic procession round the dome till the encircling frieze should be complete." (Brumidi's remaining designs were painted later by another Italian artist, Philip Costaggini, who also added several of his own. Three panels remained blank until 1951, when Allyn Coxe finished the frieze.)

Two men praised the artist in the Senate Chamber several days after Brumidi's death. "How rich the inheritance he has left to the present and succeeding ages!" Senator Voorhees of Indiana eulogized. "During more than a quarter of a century he hovered along these walls from the basement to the dome, leaving creations of imperishable beauty wherever his touch has been." Senator Morrill of Vermont remarked: "So long had he devoted his heart and strength to this Capitol that his love and reverence for it was not surpassed by even that of Michelangelo for St. Peter's."

Constantino Brumidi's grave went unmarked and was finally lost to memory. Mrs. Myrtle Cheney Murdock, a Congressman's wife who became interested in the immigrant Italian artist who had done so many paintings throughout the Capitol, finally located Brumidi's burial place within a fenced but neglected plot in a Washington cemetery. Her campaign to arouse the nation's respect and remembrance for the artist resulted in an appropriation for a suitable marker—a kindly if belated gesture from Brumidi's adopted country. Yet the now well-tended grave or even some future memorial to Brumidi can be only secondary honors. Brumidi's best monuments are preserved upon the walls and ceilings of the Capitol.

The General Commands a Museum

Luigi Palma di Cesnola

"I have the pride of my race, and that of a Discoverer
who wants his name perpetuated with his works . . ."

WARS AND FAMINE have scattered and destroyed peoples,
and the things they once made and used were covered by the
dust of time. In the last century, archeologists began to discover, unearth, and study piece by piece these artifacts from
cultures of long ago. Museums acquiring relics of mankind's
past added them to art treasures saved from more recent
centuries, then showed their priceless collections to the public—to admire, ponder over, and learn from. The Metropolitan Museum of Art in New York preserves and displays for
Americans the story of the world's civilizations recorded for
thousands of years on stone, wood, clay, metal, cloth, and
paper. The early solidarity and success of our country's largest
art museum came largely through the efforts of an Italian in
America.

Luigi Palma di Cesnola began his career in the United
States as a soldier fighting for the Union Army. (He later
received the Congressional Medal of Honor for his bravery.)

Afterward a diplomat serving his new country, as a sideline he became one of America's foremost archeologists. Finally, as the Metropolitan Museum of Art's first director for twenty-five years his knowledge, dedication, and executive ability helped to build one of the great repositories of world art.

In his peacetime professions Luigi Palma di Cesnola had many attributes of a good Army officer. He was firm, indefatigable, thorough, dignified, farseeing. He organized people and projects skillfully; he got jobs done swiftly and well; he expected obedience from those under his command. But his temper often soared when things did not proceed according to his plans; he was accused of being a dictator. Some people loved him and obeyed him implicitly; others disliked him and rebelled. Inevitably, little wars were waged around him: he always suited his title of "The General."

Wars had been part of Cesnola's early life. His father, a Piedmontese nobleman, had served with Napoleon; later he fought in the 1821 rebellion against Austrian rule, and for a time he was Minister of War for the Kingdom of Sardinia, which became the center of the Risorgimento, the unification movement in Italy. Count Cesnola's second son, Luigi, was born on June 29, 1832, at Rivarolo, near Turin. As a child he attended military schools. In 1848, when war again broke out between Austria and Sardinia, young Luigi volunteered for the Sardinian Army. When his courage at the battle of Novara in 1849 earned him a lieutenant's rank, he became the Army's youngest officer. After the war he finished his education at the Royal Military Academy. During the Crimean War he was on the staff of Sardinia's commanding general and took part in the fall of Sebastopol.

Luigi Palma di Cesnola came to New York in early 1860, just before the various Italian states, with help from the patriot Garibaldi and guidance from the statesman Cavour, achieved independence and unified, with Victor Emmanuel II of Sardinia as king. Cesnola hoped ultimately to find his fortune in America as a "scientific soldier"; in the meantime he supported himself by giving French and Italian lessons. In 1861, he married one of his students—Mary Isabel Reid, daughter of Captain Samuel Chester Reid, a Naval hero who had also designed the American flag with its thirteen permanent stripes and an increasing number of stars as states were admitted.

When the Civil War began, Cesnola, like many other Italian immigrants, offered his services to the Union Army. As a tall, stately lieutenant-colonel in the 11th New York Cavalry regiment, he recruited soldiers and became known as an expert drillmaster and disciplinarian. "In action, in speech, he was magnetic," was the way he impressed a young recruit, who later noted a unique quality which served Cesnola well in his future work: "He was endowed by nature with the power to charm others into a love for their duty."

Transferred to the 4th New York Cavalry regiment in 1862, Cesnola was made a brigade leader under the command of General Judson Kilpatrick. When another general made his own inexperienced brother Cesnola's superior officer, the Italian colonel complained of nepotism—and was arrested. In mid-June of 1863, the fierce battle at the Aldie gap in Virginia began; Cesnola's men refused to fight without him, so he was released, to lead them in three successful charges. General Kilpatrick, praising Cesnola's "heroic conduct," presented him with his own sword. On the fourth charge, Colonel Cesnola was wounded and his brigade overcome by the Confederates.

With other prisoners, Cesnola marched a hundred miles

and then was packed into a train to Richmond. There he was taken, with other Yankee officers, to the notorious Libby Prison. The commanding officer offered him better quarters and special privileges because he was a foreigner, doubtless with the expectation that he would readily switch his loyalty and provide valuable information. "I am a United States officer," said Cesnola, declining all favors.

A rebel sergeant, looking for money, roughly searched him, then ordered him to remove his boots. The Italian aristocrat refused; a servant always "performed that function" for him. Finally the soldier had to stoop and remove the Colonel's boots himself—to his disappointment finding nothing in them. These boots afterwards were Cesnola's pillow when he slept on a dank wooden floor, with no blanket or coat to cover him.

In October of 1863, the U. S. Sanitary Commission sent boxes of clothing and blankets for the prisoners at Richmond. Cesnola was made the Commissary of Distribution at Belle Isle, the internment camp for 6,000 enlisted men. He went daily to the island prison and was appalled by what he saw there. Yankee soldiers with gaunt, weary faces, with hair and beard uncut, with emaciated bodies trembling with cold and fatigue and plagued by vermin, begged him in feeble voices for food. "My heart has never been moved as it was by the condition of those men at Belle Isle," Cesnola wrote later.

The Confederate commander offered parole to Belle Isle prisoners who would make shoes for the Rebels. Cesnola warned the men that by helping the enemy they would be breaking their oaths to their government and on their return home they could be court-martialed. So when the guards came to release men for work, nobody was willing to go. Cesnola was dismissed from his Commissary post for instigating the mutiny. Confined again to Libby Prison, he was finally exchanged for a Rebel colonel in March of 1864. He returned to his regiment and took part in the Shenandoah campaign under General Sheridan's command.

As the war drew to a close, President Lincoln sent for Cesnola. Giving him the brevet or honorary commission of Brigadier General, Lincoln asked him to be the American consul on Cyprus. The post required both soldierly firmness and diplomatic skill, for the island, at a strategic spot in the eastern Mediterranean, was perpetually in political ferment, with the Greek majority at odds with their Turkish rulers. Cesnola became a United States citizen, and late in 1865 he left for his new post of duty.

On Christmas Day, the steamer carrying General Cesnola, his wife, and their baby daughter stopped a mile offshore from the harborless Larnaca—their future residence. "The town from that distance looked the very picture of desolation," Cesnola remembered. A small boat flying the Stars and Stripes drew alongside the steamer and twenty people clambered on board, wearing red fezzes and carrying antique pistols, sabers, and silver-knobbed batons. Their appearance alarmed Cesnola—especially when told they were his consular employees.

The uneasy Cesnolas and their baggage were transferred to the smaller boat, which set out for Larnaca. When the boat got stuck on a sand bar, a boatman leapt into the water and motioned for the General to perch upon his shoulders and be carried ashore; reluctantly, he did so. "It was therefore in this undiplomatic style," Cesnola later reported, "that I was obliged to make my entry into the city of Larnaca."

After meeting a number of interesting and agreeable people, the Cesnolas soon felt more cheerful about their future on Cyprus. They leased a large house along the marina, close to the consulate. Since whatever Cesnola did he did enthusiastically and thoroughly, he now studied Cypriote history. In his free hours he began to explore the remains of Citium, the ancient city close to Larnaca. He dug into many mounds, and one proved to be a ruined temple. From it, Cesnola unearthed numerous terra-cotta figures. He also explored many tombs.

His discoveries whetted his interest in archeology. He knew of the remarkable work being done by the first professional archeologists uncovering the long-lost sites of great cities in the classical world and in Asia Minor. For thousands of years Cyprus had been visited, colonized, fought over, and conquered by Phoenicians, Assyrians, Persians, Jews, Egyptians, Greeks, Romans, Arabs, Medieval crusaders, Venetians, and Turks. Ancient Cypriote art and architecture inevitably would show the changes wrought by these external peoples. Cyprus was the Mediterranean area's richest source of copper, the main ingredient in bronze—the all-important metal for weapons, tools, and pots.

A few French archeologists had explored parts of the island, and of course, through the centuries, old tombs had been plundered. Since nobody had yet approached Cypriote archeology systematically, Cesnola now pored over ancient writings and antique maps and managed to learn the accepted methods of locating and exploring ruins, of charting and preserving them for future use, of unearthing relics carefully and restoring them properly, and of photographing the stages and results of his efforts.

As he began traveling to other sites, Cesnola delegated more consular responsibilities to his assistants. He got a *firman,* an official permit from Constantinople to search for archeological remains. Unable to interest any of his friends in Europe or America to help finance his explorations, he proceeded at his own expense, regularly employing a number of native diggers.

During his first years on Cyprus, Cesnola gathered together an impressive collection of antique objects: statues, sarcophagi, vases, lamps, jewelry, copper and bronze weapons, and glass. As his success became known, the Europeans at Larnaca entered into a lively competition to find buried artifacts. Yet there had been little drama until early one morning in 1870, when a messenger arrived to say that Cesnola's diggers at Athieno—built close to the site of ancient Golgoi—had just found a colossal stone head and some other sculptures. Fearing that the peasants would seize and try to sell them, the diggers urged Cesnola to come at once with some carts. Cesnola had to attend a meeting, so he sent a consular employee in his stead. Late that evening he learned that the site was now swarming with peasants who, with pick, shovel, or bare hands, were digging to get treasures for themselves. Another messenger reported that the Turkish police had come and were claiming all the objects found as the property of the Sultan, that many peasants had hidden relics away in their huts. Cesnola mounted his horse and hurried to Athieno, several hours away.

The scene confronting him was wild and weird. "The moon was not yet risen," Cesnola recalled, "and large fires were lit at different points, throwing fantastic shadows as men moved about, eagerly gesticulating and conversing."

The American consul was known far and wide for his resolute and clever manner of handling all problems. Now, as he approached, the racket and chaos suddenly ceased. Cesnola knew exactly what to do, "having been long accus-

tomed to the control of large bodies of men during my
military life." He rode up to the two Turkish policemen and
issued orders: one was to hold his horse, the other to disperse
the crowd. Without questioning his authority, they obeyed.
Soon all was quiet and orderly. "I then saw for the first time
the colossal head," Cesnola remembered. He was impressed
and moved, briefly envisaging "a people whose master-hands
had ages long ago withered and fallen into dust." Cesnola
had the sculptures placed in his carts, then sent them off to
Larnaca. "Thus I may say that I rather captured than discovered those stone treasures," he admitted.

In the morning Cesnola purchased the site from its owner.
He also bought all the objects that the peasants had found
and hidden away the previous day. He had thirty-two statues
showing Egyptian or Assyrian influence; all were broken—
some long before, others from a hasty and improper use of
tools. Believing that a temple was nearby, Cesnola told his
diggers to excavate a mound. After days of labor they encountered a thick stone wall at the depth of seven feet; this
they followed with their spades until they exposed the four
sides of a rectangular structure thirty by sixty feet. Cesnola
had found the famous Golgoi temple dedicated to Venus.

Cesnola now employed more than a hundred diggers. Piece
by piece statues and pedestals were discovered as they carefully dug downward, softening the concrete-like clay soil with
water carried in jars from a distant spring. One large clay-
covered statue, appearing to be a bearded figure in a long
robe, seemed intact. Although the profile of this statue was
visible, there was over six feet of hardened clay to be removed
from its back. "Each blow of the pickaxe made me shiver even
in that hot climate," Cesnola said. He applied a wet sponge
to the head and with a knife and a piece of soft wood patiently

removed the clay stuck on it. "Thus I labored for days," he remembered, "gradually developing one feature after another, until the whole magnificent head was laid bare, and found unmarred by even a scratch."

Meanwhile, Cesnola's workers located another large group of statues, these in Greek and Roman styles. To prevent a rapid evaporation of moisture absorbed for centuries, all statues were put in tents; under the hot sun they would have split apart.

When the Governor-General of Cyprus heard of Cesnola's fabulous find, he ordered all digging stopped until official instructions came from Constantinople; yet at the same time he considerately lent Cesnola a dozen tents to shelter his diggers. "The incongruity of this was thoroughly Turkish," Cesnola remarked. The General feared that Turkish officials would confiscate his relics and sell them for their own profit. Unless he moved the precious sculptures at once to his Larnaca home, where they would be protected under the American flag, all his work and expenditures might be for naught. The homeward journey was long and laborious, but at last all relics were safe under Cesnola's own roof. The diggers leveled the Golgoi site and returned to their homes, happy with generous wages for several months' work.

Back at Larnaca, Cesnola faced a crisis. Turkey and Greece were on the verge of war, and the Turks had ordered the entire Greek population on Cyprus to leave within twenty days. The Greek consul asked for Cesnola's help; Greeks flocked to the American consulate for advice and even bread.

Cesnola went to Nicosia, the capital of Cyprus, to talk with the Governor-General and try to delay the order. The Greeks, he declared, would be unable to pay their debts to the Turks until after harvest time. Also, he argued, the European powers would never allow a war between Turkey and Greece. The Governor-General agreed to postpone the exodus from Cyprus; afterwards Constantinople revoked the order throughout the Turkish domain and the war clouds passed away. Thanks to the persuasive powers of the American consul, not a single Greek subject had left his Cyprus home.

Cesnola returned to his archeology. He wondered what to do with the treasures that filled his house and several nearby warehouses. His collection became a chief attraction to tourists, who insisted upon viewing it whether convenient or not to Cesnola. "I was consequently at times not a little annoyed," he said. Too, he was learning an odd and troublesome aspect of human behavior pertaining to his future museum work: "When great numbers were admitted to inspect my discoveries, it was not always possible to keep visitors from handling the small objects which were all lying on tables and shelves, and I am sorry to say that sometimes the objects did not always find their way back to their legitimate places."

Although the *firman* granted to Cesnola had given the government no claim to his findings, the Governor-General now forbade him to ship his relics out of Cyprus. Cesnola intended to give a generous selection of his antiquities to Constantinople's Ottoman Museum, but he distrusted the Turkish officials: in the past, two large crates of antiquities he had sent as gifts to the museum had never arrived there.

The General decided to get all his relics off the island as soon as possible—by force, if necessary, even requesting a man-of-war from the American Secretary of the Navy. Cesnola finally chartered a Greek vessel. Since the Larnaca customs director had special orders forbidding the exportation of anything by the American consul, Cesnola simply arranged for the friendly Russian consul to ship his collection out for him. Soon all available dock workers were carrying Cesnola's precious cargo on board the waiting ship, bound for London. His whole fortune was invested in these treasures, and they were not insured. To Cesnola's relief, his collection arrived safely in England without incident. When he heard of Cesnola's ruse, the Governor-General admitted that the whole affair had been most cleverly managed: such a pity that the General was not a Turk!

Cesnola began to offer his collection of more than 10,000 objects for sale to eminent museums. He corresponded with the British Museum and the Louvre, sending descriptions and photographs of his relics. John Taylor Johnston, the president of the Metropolitan Museum of Art in New York, also received a letter from Cesnola that introduced his Cypriote treasures: "I have the most valuable and richest private collection of antiquities existing in the world, which is the result of six years' labor, in this famous island, and of a great outlay of money." The General had read a magazine article about the new American museum founded in 1869; he much admired its intention to acquire for the United States an art collection that could stand ultimately as a respected equal beside those in European museums.

General Cesnola went to England in 1873 to prepare an exhibition of some of his Cypriote antiquities. Many renowned Englishmen wanted the British Museum to purchase his treasures. The American millionaire Cyrus W. Field enthused over the exhibit and recommended that the Metropolitan Museum buy it; consequently, Johnston offered $60,000 to Cesnola for the entire collection. For the sculptures and inscriptions from the Golgoi temple alone the British Museum had offered $50,000, which meant that Cesnola could sell his many other relics elsewhere—perhaps being able to earn as much as $200,000 from private sales.

Cesnola accepted the American museum's offer. "I did not undertake archeological diggings for a commercial profit," he explained to Johnston. "And though my collection represents today my whole fortune 'in toto,' yet I am disposed to be very reasonable when a *public* Institution would like to purchase it. What I desire above all is that my collection should remain all *together* and be know as the Cesnola Collection."

"I have the pride of my race, and that of a Discoverer who wants his name perpetuated with his works if possible," Cesnola also told Johnston. Because the Metropolitan Museum wanted all his antiquities, and because Cesnola wanted his adopted country to keep the fruits of his long labors, his Cypriote antiquities—believed at the time to be the world's oldest and most extensive collection of relics—went at a nominal cost to the world's youngest art museum. This important purchase gave the small museum an impressive reputation.

Cesnola took a leave of absence from the consulship and accompanied his collection to New York. There he supervised its uncrating, saw to repairs and restorations, and classified thousands of items. Then he arranged the Cesnola Collection into a crowded but fascinating display at the museum's temporary quarters in a mansion (while the new building in Central Park was under construction).

Cesnola returned to Cyprus in 1874 and eagerly and systematically resumed his archeological explorations. He traveled all over the island, when time permitted, to uncover buried temples, enter ancient tombs, and search for the sites of long-lost cities. A financial crisis at the Metropolitan Museum of Art prevented it from sharing his expenses, so Cesnola continued his searches with his own funds.

For some while no discovery approached the drama or value of the Golgoi temple. Then Cesnola visited Curium, an ancient city on the southwest coast of Cyprus. Inspecting the site, he found a mosaic pavement that looked like a temple floor; below it the earth sounded hollow. He ordered his diggers to excavate, and at a depth of twenty-five feet they discovered four interconnected vaults almost filled with dirt . . . but also with an astounding collection of gold and silver jewelry and other rare items—bronze lamps, vases, gems, and sculptures. Cesnola had located a temple's secret treasure vaults, concealed from the world for several thousand years.

The General might have continued for years his Cypriote explorations. But returning home to Larnaca with his new Curium treasures, he found his wife in a melancholy mood. For years she had lived far away from the sophisticated society she had known as a girl in New York; she raised their two daughters, worked happily in her garden, and encouraged her husband's archeological work—accompanying him whenever possible. But she had a constant fear of an accident befalling him during his lengthy expeditions; the recent death of an archeologist inspecting a tomb Cesnola had excavated completely unnerved her.

Cesnola recognized his duty. He resigned his post, packed up their belongings, and crated his Curium antiquities, which he sent off to the Metropolitan Museum—all but the most valuable objects, which he wanted to keep with him. With mixed feelings they departed from Cyprus, which had been their home for a dozen years and where the General had acquired new interests and a new profession. In all, he had

Southern European immigrants on an Atlantic steamship

Henri de Tonti, from a relief sculpture in the Marquette Building, Chicago, Illinois. *Below: Le Rocher* or "Starved Rock" on the Illinois River, where La Salle and Tonti built Fort St. Louis in 1683.

A miniature painting of Philip Mazzei, made in Paris in 1790. *Below:* The remains of Colle, the house near Monticello which Mazzei built in 1774.

Brumidi's allegorical painting of "The Apotheosis of Washington," in the dome of the Capitol's rotunda.

Constantino Brumidi. *Below:*
Brumidi's painting of Columbus, in the President's Room
of the Capitol.

General Luigi Palma di Cesnola

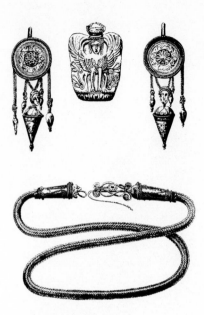

Artifacts found by Cesnola in
the "treasure vaults" at Curium on Cyprus: Gold neck-
lace, brooch, and earrings.

Above: Statue of Cypriote
priest unearthed by Cesnola
at Golgoi (6′ 3″). *Left:* Silver
plate found by Cesnola on
Cyprus.

Saint Frances Xavier Cabrini

What Mother Cabrini saw: Little Italy section in New York City

Arturo Toscanini

Toscanini conducting

A. P. Giannini

Birthplace in San Francisco in 1904 of the Bank of Italy —to become Bank of America.

Courtesy, Bank of America

Courtesy, Bank of America

A model of the new Bank of America headquarters in San Francisco.

Major Fiorello
La Guardia, 1918

Enrico Fermi

Fiorello H.
La Guardia

The tenth layer of Fermi's atomic pile, showing dark cylinders of uranium ore imbedded in graphite blocks upon a wooden support. The pile eventually had fifty-seven layers. *Below:* The first atomic pile or nuclear reactor, built by Fermi in 1942 at the University of Chicago.

found more than 35,000 objects while exploring sixty-five necropoli (with at least 60,000 tombs) and twenty-three other sites on the island.

The Cesnolas stayed in England in 1877, before returning to New York. There General Louis Palma di Cesnola wrote a book about Cypriote history that also described his own experiences and explorations: *Cyprus—Its Ancient Cities, Tombs, and Temples.* Published in both England and the United States, it was very popular; in America it increased the public's interest in the Cesnola Collection at the Metropolitan Museum.

Back in New York, General Cesnola devoted full time to the museum, at first cataloguing his new group of antiquities and preparing them for exhibition. He made such an excellent impression upon the museum's trustees that he was elected Secretary of the Metropolitan Museum, a position he held for the rest of his life. Soon afterwards, he was made its first director and he began to receive a salary.

Cesnola's first important duty as director was to supervise the removal of the museum's art collection to its permanent new home at Fifth Avenue and Eighty-second Street in Central Park. At the time, the building seemed large; today it is only the small, central part of an enormous, sprawling structure. Day and night Cesnola worked; he wrote memoranda of work to be done, directed the crating of all the treasures, mapped out display locations in the new quarters, and hired trustworthy assistants.

On March 30, 1880, the Metropolitan Museum of Art was declared open to the public. In the official fanfare U. S. President Rutherford B. Hayes gave a speech of greeting. Then one of the museum's officers, Joseph H. Choate, told the assembled wealthy guests of the trustees' plan for the

American museum: "To convert your useless gold into things of living beauty that shall be a joy to a whole people for a thousand years."

Cesnola and his Cypriote art were comfortably settled into the museum. The General had a few assistants, but the real running of the Metropolitan, with its many details and responsibilities and decisions, was largely his. The museum's artistic and financial success in the early years was primarily due to Cesnola's unceasing devotion. He was hard-working, diplomatic, enthusiastic, scholarly, painstaking with all details, economy-minded, and ambitious and imaginative in his plans for the museum's future. In short, he was indispensable. He had a genius for organizing people, for getting things done.

Since wealthy men had confidence in Cesnola's administrative abilities and responded to his eager plans, they opened their pocketbooks to help the museum pay its expenses or buy new treasures, and from time to time they offered it prize *objets d'art* and paintings from their own fabulous private collections. "The Museum is growing rapidly by donation and purchase," Cesnola noted with satisfaction in 1882, "and holds out promise of speedily becoming one of the great museums of the world, not only in the value and rarity of special features, but in completeness and symmetry. America has long waited for such a comprehensive collection, and the time seems to have come when the hopes of the lovers and students of the history of Art will be speedily fulfilled."

But there were those who resented Cesnola's directorship, some perhaps because of his authoritarian manner of marshaling his employees and making decisions, others because they disagreed with his policies and his taste in art and themselves coveted his position. Their hostility soon found a focus. In August of 1880, *The Art Amateur* published an article written by Gaston L. Feaurdent, a dealer in antiques who had kept the Cesnola Collection when it first arrived in London. He charged that some of Cesnola's antiquities had been fraudulently restored, by the General himself or under his direction; therefore Cesnola was duping both the museum's trustees and the admiring public.

Cesnola leapt to defend his honor and the authenticity of his Cypriote collection. He published a "brief and total denial" of the charges and called his attacker a "public slanderer" whose own archeology was "charlatanism." He believed that Feaurdent's article was the start of a plot to dislodge him from his post as director of the Metropolitan Museum. The General's ire and disgust at first knew no bounds. His friends finally persuaded him to cease his public abuse of his foe.

As Cesnola prepared for the thorough examination of both his integrity and his Cypriote relics, he was assured that all the museum's trustees stood behind him. They appointed a committee of investigation—two trustees and three art experts—to judge on the authenticity of his collection. After several months of careful study the committee released its report: all Feaurdent's charges were "without foundation" and there was nothing "to cast a shadow" on the merit of the Cesnola Collection at the museum.

General Cesnola's reputation was vindicated only for a while. In 1882, a pamphlet written by an art critic for the New York *Tribune,* Clarence Cook, repeated Feaurdent's charges and also declared that two of Cesnola's statues were a "fraudulent patchwork of unrelated parts." In reply, the museum removed the statues from their cases, put them in the main hall, and invited the public to examine them. During the following weeks the two statues underwent a variety of tests contrived by experienced sculptors and scholars and also by curious amateurs. They were peered at through magnifying glasses, scrubbed with chemicals, scraped, gouged, shaken, and pounded upon. Everybody concluded that the statues were quite genuine indeed.

But this did not end Cesnola's woes. Feaurdent, who had blistered under the General's denouncement, now sued him for $25,000, charging a defamation of his character as an art and archeological expert. The New York papers chose up sides as the notorious libel trial began on October 31, 1883. For months the Cesnola-Feaurdent controversy was a leading news item; the public followed Feaurdent's angry charges, then Cesnola's dignified defense. Attendance at the museum increased with all the publicity. Again supporting their director, the trustees also insisted upon paying his legal expenses. On February 2, 1884, after twenty-eight hours of deliberation, the jury decided in defendant Cesnola's favor.

On several later occasions Cesnola and his Cypriote collection came under mild attacks. But never again would the General have to undergo a noisy public debate over his honor. Expert examinations subsequently have upheld the Cesnola Collection's authenticity.

The Metropolitan Museum thrived under Cesnola's diligent care. In its first year in Central Park the value of its collections was about a half-million dollars; only eight years later it was two and a quarter million dollars. In an avalanche of bestowed treasures, the museum received gifts that represented the arts for centuries past from all corners of the world: paintings, sculptures, medieval tapestries and armor, precious porcelains, lace work, costumes, antique musical instruments, gems, coins, rare books, maps, and manuscripts.

J. Pierpont Morgan, the art-loving financier who served for years as a trustee, then as the museum's president, was among the wealthy patrons giving money and their own possessions to the Metropolitan. A very welcome bequest came from an inconspicuous annual member who made the museum the residuary legatee of his five million dollar estate, with the provision that the income be spent only for the purchase of new works of art.

Other gifts were less acceptable—like a proferred assemblage of "monkeys in various materials." General Cesnola was often contacted by needy people who asked the museum to buy some "rare" item from them. One lady offered for sale a painting of St. Michael slaying the dragon, which, she said, her great-grandfather had unearthed in the ancient Roman city of Herculaneum. Cesnola wrote back, unable to resist irony: "Herculaneum has been lying under the lava of Vesuvius for 2,000 years. That the canvas should have escaped destruction when the mountain poured forth its fiery contents on the towns at its base is indeed remarkable. . . . That the artist should have shown a spirit of prophecy and delineated an incident of the Christian religion long before it happened is more than remarkable. It is miraculous. You should keep the Saint Michael."

Cesnola kept a balanced budget. ("Debt is to be avoided as the King of terrors," he declared.) Meanwhile, New York City steadily increased its subsidy for operating and expanding the museum. In 1888, a new wing was added, but almost as soon as it opened, the need for more space became apparent. During Cesnola's long tenure four new wings were built. Finding the collection too large and varied for him to oversee personally in all aspects, he decided to introduce the British Museum's plan of appointing curators or specialists to head particular departments of art. When Cesnola first adopted the curatorial system in 1886 there were three curators; today there are ten.

Since there was never enough room for displaying all the museum's possessions as well as loan exhibitions, many of Cesnola's Cypriote antiquities stayed in storage. In 1886, a number of duplicates or near-duplicates were sold to Leland Stanford, California's millionaire governor. The money from this sale was used to purchase Egyptian antiquities from the Cairo Museum, thus starting the Metropolitan's great collection of Egyptian art. Cesnola's pride no longer depended on having his relics all together; he recognized that by selling items to other museums, people throughout the country would be able to view the objects he had found in Cyprus. (After his death several auctions of Cesnola's antiques were held, and the museum's profit from the sales was many times over what it had originally paid Cesnola; and still the museum itself retains the finest collection of Cypriote art outside of Cyprus.)

Like other nineteenth-century institutions, the Metropolitan Museum was resolutely closed on Sundays. However, as the Christian interpretation of the day of rest changed, pressure mounted for the museum to open its doors on Sundays. In May of 1891, the officers finally gave in to the public's demands. During the last half of the year Sunday visitors made up a third of the full year's attendance—proving the museum's value as an educational and recreational place for working-class people. General Cesnola at first could not be reconciled to these Sunday crowds; they seemed, he said, to expect the Metropolitan to provide freaks and monstrosities, like the Dime Museums on the Bowery. But within a short time the thrill-seekers and object-handlers, the pickpockets and the vandals, either disappeared—or changed into people whom the General found "respectable, law-abiding, and intelligent." Cesnola already realized, of course, that the museum had inestimable value as an educational experience. "Teaching," he said, "is better done by object than by word."

Although General Cesnola gave much of his time and energy to his museum, he was also a devoted husband and father. He had inherited the title of Count, but preferred to remain known as General. His wife, who moved with her illustrious husband among New York society's elite, was called Countess Cesnola and made up for her dreary years on Cyprus by leading an active social career and working for charitable causes.

The General gathered honors by the dozens. He had memberships in many of the world's literary and scientific societies. Princeton and Columbia Universities gave him honorary degrees. And his Italian homeland had scarcely forgotten him: Italian kings conferred knightly orders upon him and had two medals specially struck for him. When Cesnola returned to Italy in 1900, the newspapers followed his itinerary as though he were a conquering hero. In 1897, Cesnola received the decoration that made him particularly proud: the Congressional Medal of Honor, the highest award given by the United States government, presented to him some thirty years after an act of bravery in the Civil War.

As he grew older, Cesnola's pace hardly slowed. The museum was always his principal interest, and after his wife's death he spent most of his waking hours there. The aging General—with his hair iron-gray, his walrus mustache ever luxuriant, his dark eyes still lively and commanding and all-seeing behind his glasses, his tall frame holding a good military posture—was the Metropolitan Museum's most important possession.

But times were changing around Cesnola. Some people felt that he was not keeping up with them, that his taste still belonged to the nineteenth century. Also, he insisted that his museum, like the army, should not employ women—a rule finally broken in 1896 by the hiring of a female assistant curator.

Luigi Palma di Cesnola died on November 20, 1904, after a brief illness, at the age of seventy-two. "The Museum as we know it today may be regarded as a monument to his energy, enterprise, and rare executive skill," said the *Scientific American*—noting too that it would be hard to replace him.

Someday when you visit the huge Metropolitan Museum of Art in New York it will assume a more intimate aspect if you imagine that the General accompanies you on your tour. He walks with dignity up the wide stairs, enters a gallery to study the paintings, reads inscriptions here, admires statues there. He makes a thorough inspection: the guards must be wide-awake, the glass cases dusted, all correct and in order. Yet, meanwhile, your ghostly companion may be thinking: an individual creates and then dies; his culture too comes to an end; but so long as Mankind makes things beautiful and useful, so long as it searches out, preserves, and cherishes the records of its past, there is immortality in each of us.

A Saint Among the Immigrants

Francesca Xavier Cabrini

"Let your lives be a perennial sacrifice of yourselves in behalf of the human race."

LEGENDS SURROUND even her birth. On July 15, 1850, a flock of pure white doves—never seen before or since in Sant' Angelo Lodigiano in Lombardy—settled in the fields of Agostino Cabrini. To shoo them away from his ripening wheat, the farmer swung a threshing flail. One dove got caught, and Agostino gently set it free. Just then, within his house, his thirteenth and last child was born.

A frail infant born two months early in a family where only three children had survived, Maria Francesca Cabrini was all the more precious—and feared likely to depart soon. She was taken on the day of her birth to the village church and baptized. Sister Rosa, older by a dozen years, took charge of "Cecchina"—the little one—since their parents were in their fifties and too busy to give their new baby constant attention. She dressed her small sister and took her daily to church; she taught her to read and write; she scolded her for any neglect of rules or duties. Cecchina thrived, without losing her gentle and joyous nature or resenting and rebelling against Rosa's strict regime. Her childhood was a known and orderly world within whose confines she had peace, security, and purpose. "Regulations are helpful," Francesca was to write later, "not only to Religious but to everyone, for human nature is prone to tire, relax, and change according to events."

Cecchina was obedient; but she was also lively and imaginative, and loved solitude. Now and again she escaped her sister's surveillance and stole away, to sail paper boats down a nearby stream. The stream would come to a river; the river would flow to the sea; and the sea would lead to faraway China. In her boats Cecchina put flowers—missionaries whom she was sending abroad. (Francesca had often listened to her uncle-priest's stories of dedicated saints who had given their lives to bringing Christianity to heathens in far-off lands.) The stream would indeed lead to a river, and the river to a great ocean. And across that ocean in stout boats many times Mother Cabrini and her missionary daughters would sail. Not to the China of her young dreams, but to the New World, to America, that called so many Italians to earn bread for their families.

As a child, Francesca Cabrini showed an extraordinary piety. She later recalled her feelings during her early confirmation: "I seemed no longer on earth. My heart was replete with the most pure joy. I cannot say what I felt, but I know it was the Holy Ghost." Her joy in her faith expanded; she communed with God daily in her solitary prayers. Already she had consecrated her life to serving Him. In her home, faith in God and Church was devout, simple, unquestioned—part of the very air that she breathed.

For five years Francesca attended the school of the Daughters of the Sacred Heart at Arluno, and in 1868 she received a teacher's certificate. Although she asked to enter the convent as a postulant, she was rejected because of her poor health. She was told that nun's bodies must be as strong as their souls, to be able to perform the hard tasks of their vocation.

Francesca stayed at home for several years, caring for her aged parents, managing the household, and helping Rosa and her brother in the farm work. After her parents' deaths, she became a teacher in nearby Vidardo. There she met Don Antonio Serrati, who would be her spiritual guide for years. Hardier now and experienced in teaching, Francesca applied for admission to several convents, yet again she was refused. When Serrati became a Monsignor in Codogno, he sent for Francesca to come and work at the House of Providence. Its owner, Antonia Tondini, received a stipend from the diocese for keeping an orphanage; ill-tempered, slovenly, capricious, she and her assistant were the despair of the local churchmen. Monsignor Serrati, knowing Francesca Cabrini's inner strength, her liking for work, her sound judgment, and her rapport with children, believed that the small and frail woman might work miracles. For six years Francesca stayed at the orphanage, enduring insults, physical abuse, the lack of elementary comforts and privacy. In a crucial trial for both flesh and spirit, she sometimes weakened. "I wept a great deal," she later confessed.

In 1874, Monsignor Serrati allowed Francesca Cabrini and two of the orphanage girls to become novices. On September 13, 1877, she took her final vows. When Serrati appointed her Mother Superior of the orphanage, her conflicts with Antonia Tondini became even worse. Finally the orphanage was dissolved, and Serrati asked Mother Cabrini to start a missionary order for nuns. Mother Cabrini and seven young nuns, all girls she had befriended and trained at the orphanage, made an abandoned Franciscan friary their first home.

The Missionary Sisters of the Sacred Heart opened their first institute with makeshift furnishings, eating utensils shared, no candles for the night, and little money for food or materials. In the future many of their houses were started in a similar way. Yet what they lacked in worldly goods would always be found somehow so that their work could be done. On November 14, 1880, Monsignor Serrati said the first Mass in the improvised chapel that displayed a picture of the Sacred Heart—Jesus pointing to his human heart that loved and wished to help his fellow men. For Mother Cabrini's order, the Sacred Heart made a good symbol: her work for the glory of God served man; and the loving labor she did for man praised God.

The missionary institute operated a school, convent, orphanage, and needlecraft training center at Codogno. Never forgetting her own rejection, Mother Cabrini often accepted as postulants girls with religious natures who had been turned down by other orders; she proved uniquely able to mold them into dedicated nuns. Soon her order was asked to found schools and orphanages in neighboring towns. In 1884 they opened an academy in Milan, Lombardy's capital; by 1887 the Missionary Sisters had seven houses successfully operating.

And now it was time to travel to Rome. Mother Cabrini wanted the Vatican's approval for her young institute and its rules; she also wished to have a house in Rome itself and then start missionary activity overseas. Both Monsignor Serrati and the Bishop of Milan advised her not to go to Rome. Who in the Holy City would notice her? Yet Mother

Cabrini resolutely packed her suitcase and boarded the train for Rome with one of the sisters.

She knew nothing of the elaborate, time-consuming procedures attending any business with the Vatican. Naive, enthusiastic, daring, she spoke simply and candidly. Within three days she got an interview with Cardinal-Vicar Parocchi, who was also from Lombardy.

The Cardinal looked at the small, thin nun with bright blue eyes, who was speaking so earnestly of starting a house in Rome that could be the last stepping-stone to the world lying outside Italy, in need of her order's helping hands. Where were Mother Cabrini's letters of recommendation? he asked. Why should her little institute want to compete with the many older orders of religious men and women already doing the Church's work in Rome? Did her order have anything unique about it? . . . Mother Cabrini gazed serenely at the Cardinal. She said she could not describe this special quality; she was still just discovering it. Yet she felt confident that her nuns could accomplish many good works if he gave them a chance.

Cardinal Parocchi found this guileless and determined nun a pleasant contrast to most petitioners. She reminded him of those people of strong Christian faith from centuries before, who simply set out to help their fellow men in the name of God, many of them becoming saints. But the Cardinal quickly banished his thoughts of saints and returned to his accustomed irony. He would give Mother Cabrini permission to establish a Roman house as soon as she raised enough money. How much money? Oh, half a million *lire*. . . . Not in her whole lifetime could this tiny religious in her black habit collect that sum. The interview was clearly over.

As Mother Cabrini rose to go, the Cardinal advised her, kindly, to return to Lombardy.

Yet Mother Cabrini persisted; she had a second talk with the Cardinal. Confessing that he did not know what to do with her, she suggested that he ask the Holy Father. A preposterous notion, perhaps, but it made an indelible impression. Maybe he would tell the Pope about this forceful little nun who was supremely confident of God's will in her behalf. Mother Cabrini stayed in Rome and waited. Several weeks later Cardinal Parocchi summoned her; she was to found not one house in Rome, but two—both schools in poverty-ridden areas. This first, signal recognition of her order by the Vatican gave Mother Cabrini hope that her nuns soon could become real missionaries. Receiving financial help from the amazed Monsignor Serrati, she quickly had her two houses in Rome smoothly working.

Within six months the institute's rules had gained the Vatican Council's initial favor. Cardinal Parocchi arranged for a private interview with the Holy Father which began the long and sympathetic friendship between Mother Cabrini and elderly Pope Leo XIII, who was known as the "workingman's pope" because of his desire to better the living and working conditions of the lower classes.

Many Italians were emigrating to North and South America, and both the Catholic Church and the Italian government worried over their fate. The Italian immigrants in previous years—educated people or skilled artisans—could take care of themselves. But the *contadini,* the peasants, whom famine, drought, and poverty were driving from their homeland in a mass migration, were not prepared for radical changes in their lives. In the *Mezzogiorno*—southern Italy— particularly there was little work that farm laborers could do for pay. So to America they went for work, at first by the thousands, then by the tens of thousands, finally by the hundreds of thousands. Among those who emigrated to the United States, many moved across the continent—building railroads, mining coal, working in logging camps, growing produce, catching fish. But even more stayed in port cities and within the "Little Italy" colonies themselves those from the same town or region clustered together, re-establishing the familiar *campanilismo*—the pure localism of the people dwelling within sight and sound of the village campanile.

Italians in American cities usually dwelled in the dark, congested slum tenements. And, as one of them wrote in a plaint read to Italy's Chamber of Deputies: "Here we live like animals; one lives and dies without a priest, without teachers and without doctors." The government of Italy could do little to protect its many lowly citizens living abroad under a different civil rule. But the Catholic Church, international in its connections and altruistic in spirit, could do very much indeed.

Priests, teachers, and doctors for Italians: they required the building of churches, schools, orphanages, and hospitals. Bishop Scalabrini founded the Congregation of St. Charles Borromeo and sent its members to the United States to help the Italian immigrants there. But one small order of priests could hardly alleviate the deplorable conditions they encountered. When the Bishop met Mother Cabrini, he told her that she and her missionary nuns belonged in America. But he failed to convince her. She still wanted to go to China, the land of her childhood dreams. Still, Bishop Scalabrini wrote to New York's Cardinal Corrigan to tell him about Mother Cabrini; she was invited to come over and start an orphanage.

Mother Cabrini was ready for missionary work, but she did not yet believe that America was the right place. She took her problem to the Pope. "Go, my daughter," he advised. "But not to the East. To the West. That is where you are really needed." So to the West, to the Americas, Mother Cabrini and her Missionary Sisters of the Sacred Heart would go—to bring to the Italian poor the security, ethics, and consolation of the religion of their birth; to establish schools that would bridge the wide gulf between old culture and new, orphanages for homeless children, and hospitals for the ills of the body.

Mother Cabrini chose six nuns to go with her. They had little money but were well supplied with letters from Vatican officials. In March of 1889 they embarked for New York. The Pope had paid their fares across the Atlantic. Thus, Mother Cabrini's first missionary boat was launched on the world's great ocean by the Supreme Pontiff himself: little Cecchina surely had never imagined such glory ahead of her.

The sisters, suffering from seasickness, could hardly eat or move about or attend to devotional duties. Their frail Mother General, however, ignored the ship's swaying and visited the emigrants who were crowded into steerage, the cheapest traveling class, and were homesick, seasick, fearful, unwashed, and poorly fed. Going calmly and reassuringly among them, Mother Cabrini did what she could to tend the sick, wash and feed the children, and bolster up sinking spirits. Now and again she went up on deck to gaze at the sky's vast horizon. "It is the image of the love of God when it takes possession of a soul and makes it capable of an immensity of holy deeds," she felt.

On the last day of March, the ship docked at New York. Released at last from the customs inspection, the weary nuns were taken by two of Bishop Scalabrini's priests for an Italian dinner at their rectory. The seven nuns appreciated the welcome, but what they really needed now was rest. Where was their new home? The priests broke the bad news: the building for the orphanage that Archbishop Corrigan had asked them to start was not yet found.

The sisters took lodgings in a nearby rooming house. But they could not sleep, for their straw beds were infested with lice, and rats scurried about the room. Mother Cabrini sat in a chair all night, praying for strength to face the present crisis and pursue the difficult tasks ahead.

Next day Mother Cabrini went to see Archbishop Corrigan. A smiling Irishman, his cheerful countenance fled when he met the perturbed little Italian nun. Why was there no building ready for them? Well, he said, Countess Cesnola had found a place for them on East Fifty-ninth Street, but it was in a fashionable quarter of town, quite unsuitable for an orphanage for Italian immigrants' children. So he had forbidden the Countess to prepare it, although she had already raised several thousand dollars for Mother Cabrini's new orphanage.

Anyway, the Archbiship went on, there was little the sisters could do in New York. They had arrived much earlier than expected; they could not speak English; and missionary work among the Italian poor would be difficult, even dangerous, for such innocent and unworldly women. What Mother Cabrini and her nuns should do now, he suggested, was get on a ship and return to Italy. . . .

Mother Cabrini was greatly disturbed. She showed him her letters from the Vatican, which definitely assigned her to New York. Surely there was something she and her missionaries could do in the colony of 40,000 Italians, whose number increased weekly as more immigrants arrived.

Archbishop Corrigan reconsidered. He and his priests, most of them born in Ireland or of Irish parentage, understood the uncertainties and indignities now troubling the Italians; they too had emigrated en masse and were often ill-received because they were Catholics. Yet many of the Irish priests simply did not know what to do with their new Italian parishioners, whose expectations from their religion were quite different from their own. And there were few Italian priests in the United States who could assist them in hearing confessions and helping their countrymen with their problems.

But the Protestant churches actively proselytized among the Italians. Concerned about the living conditions in the slums, they were starting settlement houses in Italian neighborhoods, where they welcomed the immigrants and gave their children a place to play and also to learn more about America. On Sundays many Italians began to attend the Protestant services.

Archbishop Corrigan realized that if the Church was to keep its own souls and save new ones, if the faith was to remain strong—even to survive in America at all—something would have to be done about the thousands of Italians living in congestion and squalor, in confusion and fear. Here before him now was this frail but resolute nun who came all the way from Italy believing she could work wonders in America. Well, let her try. As a start, Mother Cabrini could give catechism classes to Italian children at St. Joachim's Church near Mulberry Street.

Mother Cabrini had placed one foot in the doorway of America. Several weeks later she went with Countess Cesnola to see Archbishop Corrigan again. Together they implored him to allow them to prepare the orphanage. Mother Cabrini had seen the homeless children, whose mothers had died or abandoned them, whose fathers were far away in mines or logging camps or on railroad crews. They wore rags for clothing, got food from garbage cans, and slept in the dirty, dark, and cold hallways of tenements. When she described them, the Archbishop relented. She could have her orphanage.

Mother Cabrini now set her two feet firmly on American soil. The catechism classes in the church basement grew into a regular parochial school for Italian children. "It is in your hands to form new generations," Mother Cabrini told her teacher-nuns, "to lead them in the right direction, to instill into them those principles which are the seed of good works."

The orphanage on Fifty-ninth Street was soon filled with the happy noise of children with a home. On its opening day Mother Cabrini had found a loaf of bread beside the statue of the Sacred Heart—a sure sign to her that God would provide. God did provide . . . with Mother Cabrini's help. Daily, she and her nuns, carrying large baskets, rode the trolley down to Mulberry Street, where they went from shop to shop, asking the Italian proprietors for food, clothing, and money for the orphans. They always returned with their baskets full.

Mother Cabrini also began other missionary work—not among the heathens, but among her fellow Italians who lived in the tenements of Little Italy. Many immigrants felt trapped and unhappy in America, where the cold winter climate and the lack of fresh air, sunshine, and good food undermined their health. Yet they had jobs; they celebrated every saint's day with a *festa* and found other ways to make their lives more pleasant. Many men who first came over alone managed to save enough money to bring over wives, children, and parents—to reunite the family. But often too busy, too tired, too confused, or feeling unwelcome at church services not in their own language, they were abandoning their religious practices and neglecting to have their children raised properly in their faith. Mother Cabrini believed that the church was the salvation for these straying and despairing souls. "Take religion away from man," she said, "and nothing remains in this life but illusion, trials, and afflictions without number."

Now Mother Cabrini fully understood why Pope Leo XIII had sent her to the United States. Here she was truly needed. There was much work to be done; but hard work never bothered Mother Cabrini. "When things are easy, everything appears to smile," she said; "but difficulties prove where there is fidelity and constancy." And she advised her nuns: "Let your lives be a perennial sacrifice of yourselves in behalf of the human race." She had observed something about her own physical frailty: when she was working, she was well; when a task was over, she became ill. The solution?—"I must get up and look for more work."

As soon as the school and orphanage could function without her, Mother Cabrini returned to Italy to get more nuns. At Codogno, to celebrate the tenth anniversary of the founding of the Missionary Sisters of the Sacred Heart, she described the lot of the Italian immigrants in New York and aroused in her nuns a keen desire to assist her there. Then in Rome, Mother Cabrini told the Pope about her American experiences.

In April of 1890 she returned to New York with seven missionary sisters. She went at once to see a large estate in the Peekskills above the Hudson River, which the Jesuits were offering for sale at a low price, since they had not found a water source. Mother Cabrini had dreamed of finding a place in the country to which several hundred orphans could be moved, and where she might eventually set up a novitiate or training school for her nuns. She determined to buy the property. Water could be brought up the steep slope from the river below.

Now, if ony she could get enough money for a down payment. . . . Mother Cabrini prayed long and fervently—and begged relentlessly for funds among rich and poor. Few people could ever resist Mother Cabrini's persuasive and practical pleading: she got her estate and named it West Park.

Soon after the orphanage was moved, Mother Cabrini took a walk through the woods at West Park and noticed a damp spot on the ground. When a hole was dug there, a pool of water swiftly formed. The well dug at the spot took care of all their needs for water. Some of Mother Cabrini's miracles may have happened because she was observant and commonsensical.

In the fall of 1890, the Mother General was off again to Italy, this time to train sisters for a school to be opened in Nicaragua—the first of many houses she would found for the large Italian populations in Central and South America. By 1891, there were fifty Missionary Sisters of the Sacred Heart in the New World—but hardly enough for Mother Cabrini's work. In Italy and America her call sounded out for more recruits.

Mother Cabrini now responded to another worthy cause. Bishop Scalabrini's order was operating a hospital for Italians in New York; but, badly managed and poorly equipped, it was failing. When the Bishop asked her to put her nuns into

work at the hospital, she declined: they had not been trained
as nurses; furthermore, she did not want to place her order
under another's authority. Although the Vatican urged her
to enter hospital work in America, she still was reluctant.
Privately, she felt a repugnance for nursing the sick and
dying—a weakness she admitted to herself but could not seem
to overcome. Then one night she dreamed that the Virgin
Mary was performing those nursing tasks which she did not
want to do. Her attitude changed overnight. Some of her
sisters would be trained now as nurses, and she herself would
devote every effort to help ailing Italians in America.

Despite Mother Cabrini's assistance, the hospital in New
York still faltered. She then decided to found another hospital for Italians under the direction of her own order. Rent-
ing two adjoining houses on Twelfth Street, she opened her
hospital in September of 1892, with only $250 in funds and
the promised services of several doctors. They depended upon
donations for medicine, equipment, and furnishings. Their
first patients slept in beds for which mattresses and sheets
were homemade; but they got efficient, sympathetic, Italian-
speaking nurses.

Mother Cabrini was criticized for starting her hospital in
a slapdash way. Anticlerical Italians at first resented the new
hospital; for years they had been raising money for an Italian
hospital to be named after Garibaldi, but the project was
never realized because of factional differences and the absence of a strong directive staff. By wisely calling her new
clinic Columbus Hospital, Mother Cabrini honored all
Italians whether religious or not, and thus softened resistance
toward her. General Cesnola was then able to transfer the
funds for the Garibaldi Hospital to the Columbus; better
equipment was purchased, and the hospital no longer had to

depend entirely on gifts. Friendly doctors often sent paying patients to help offset the charity cases, and the Italian consul paid the hospital for treating Italian sailors. It was soon apparent to most Italians in New York that Mother Cabrini and her nuns had found another important way to aid the Italian immigrants.

But what about Italians in other American cities? Many were living in the South, working on farms, doing labor they knew and liked in a climate that was more Mediterranean. Mother Cabrini visited New Orleans, whose Archbishop asked her to start a mission there. She sent down two nuns from New York to start preparations, and she herself soon followed. She bought a large tenement on St. Philip's Street and converted it into a convent with a chapel. Its large courtyard would be used for the Italian community's social affairs. She also started a parochial school and an orphanage. In organizing her many activities there and, later, in other cities, Mother Cabrini found her New York experience very helpful.

Time and time again, Mother Cabrini personally launched complex missionary ventures in new places. Up and down the coasts of Latin America and in one American city after another she founded missions to help the Italians. Mother Cabrini was in Rome in 1900 at the celebration of Pope Leo XIII's ninetieth birthday. "Ah, Cabrini, you have the spirit of God," he greeted her. "Now carry it to the whole world." Some of that world yet awaited her.

Thirty-seven times Mother Cabrini crossed the Atlantic, each time returning to America with more missionary sisters for the ever-expanding work in schools, community missions, hospitals, and orphanages. An American novitiate was started at West Park; the thriving Columbus Hospital in New York moved to a new location; new missions were established in Chicago, Newark, Arlington. And Mother Cabrini went from one place to another, raising funds, choosing locations and staffs, inspecting, encouraging, advising, and—when necessary—admonishing. During her frequent travels to Europe, she opened up academies in Paris, Madrid, Turin, and London. Although the poor and simple people most in need of her help were closest to her heart, Mother Cabrini yet recognized that the children in wealthy families also needed religious guidance and good educations.

The United States continued to receive much of Mother Cabrini's attention: it was her first foreign mission and she was especially worried about the Italians there. In 1903, the Archbishop of Chicago asked her to start a hospital in his city. After months of strenuous fund raising, Mother Cabrini decided to buy the once-fashionable North Shore Hotel for the hospital building. In the real estate transactions she showed that basic peasant wariness which so often prevented unscrupulous people from cheating her. The owners had assured her that all the park property surrounding the hotel was included in the purchase price of $160,000. But Mother Cabrini asked several nuns to go out in the early morning to measure the dimensions of the lot. When she went to sign the purchase deed, she noticed that it specified smaller dimensions: the owners were holding out a portion of the property to sell off later. Faced with Mother Cabrini's knowledge of their deception, they hurriedly made corrections.

Mother Cabrini was out of town while the large building underwent remodeling, but returned at once when told that the contractors were doing unnecessary demolition and were overcharging for labor and materials. Mother Cabrini fired them and refused to pay their fraudulent bills; she herself

took over superintending the work. The workmen were so inspired by her zeal that they finished the remodeling ahead of
schedule. Meanwhile, Mother Cabrini secured an excellent
medical staff. Within a short time after its opening, the
Columbus Hospital earned such a fine reputation that it had
outgrown its original purpose: to provide hospitalization for
the Italian poor.

The Far West was now calling for Mother Cabrini. She
went first to Washington state, where a number of Italians
had settled, attracted by available work on farms and railroads and in fisheries and lumber camps. In Seattle, since
they did not have their own church, many had stopped going
to Mass. Mother Cabrini built a small wooden church, and
was rewarded. "It is very touching," she wrote, "to see men
of advanced years cry with emotion at seeing an Italian
church in which they hear the Word of God in their mother
tongue and are reminded of the old country." Mother
Cabrini's way of getting her people back to God always involved "a little kindness and courtesy."

Soon Mother Cabrini went off to conquer southern California, where many Italians had found its warm climate
congenial, its soil rich and productive. For them and their
children Mother Cabrini started a school, an orphanage, and
a sanatorium. Colorado became another center for her work,
for there many Italians worked in the mines and on railroads,
living in camps far away from their families and churches.
Mother Cabrini and her nuns fearlessly descended thousands
of feet into dark mine shafts, to talk with the men as they
worked and to bring them renewed contact with their religion; to help their wives and children in Denver, Mother
Cabrini established a mission. Clearly and sadly Mother
Cabrini observed the fate of so many of her countrymen in

America: "Here the hardest labor is reserved for the Italian worker. There are few who regard him with a sympathetic eye, who care for him or remember that he has a heart and soul: they merely look upon him as an ingenious machine for work."

When Mother Cabrini returned to Italy in 1906, she had become an international personage. She was celebrating, a year belatedly, the twenty-fifth anniversary of the founding of her order—which now had missions in eight countries, a total of fifty houses, and a thousand sisters. The Queen of Italy decorated her for her work. Even the politicians, usually suspicious of allowing the Catholic Church any part in the government's business, recognized that Mother Cabrini was doing more for the Italian emigrants throughout the Americas than all their efforts combined: and often they subsidized her missions. The Italian ambassador to the United States said: "I consider the illustrious Mother General of the Missionary Sisters a priceless collaborator; for while I work for the interest of Italy among the powerful, she succeeds in making it loved and esteemed by the humble, the infirm, and the children."

Mother Cabrini got malaria in Brazil in 1908 and never fully recovered. But of course she kept on working ceaselessly. On returning to the United States, she opened a second hospital in Chicago, for the exclusive use of the Italian poor. In Seattle, in 1909, she became a naturalized citizen of the United States, knowing that citizenship would give her certain advantages in her transactions.

Meanwhile Mother Cabrini was growing weary of her many worldly responsibilities. "If I followed my secret desires," she confessed, "I would go to West Park and there, far from all distractions, do many beautiful things for the Institute." But God asked for work, not meditation.

In her sixtieth year she tried to resign the Mother Generalship, but neither the Vatican nor her many nuns were willing to relieve her of her awesome duties. Mother Cabrini often had urged obedience on her daughters, and now she herself submitted meekly but wearily to their wishes. Although her health grew ever more precarious, her journeys and projects did not decrease. She inspected Europe once more; she planned a larger Columbus Hospital for New York. And she herself went to Los Angeles to salvage wood, pipes, and nails when an amusement park was razed. Using them to build an annex for her Los Angeles mission, she shipped the surplus off to Denver: Mother Cabrini never wasted anything. Then she spent a half-year in Seattle, arranging to buy a large hotel for use as a hospital. When war came to Europe, Mother Cabrini grew depressed, thinking of Lombardy under attack by the Germans. She directed all her European houses to take in orphans and feed soldiers.

Toward the end of 1916, Mother Cabrini went to Los Angeles to rest. She told enchanting stories to the orphanage children, worked in the garden, and fed the birds. In early spring she left for Chicago, where the sisters despaired of her health. But sick as she was, she scurried about—buying a farm that would provide fresh food for her missions, and attending social functions at her hospitals.

For Christmas Mother Cabrini ordered new habits for all her nuns. She spent the last evening of her life wrapping candy for school children. On December 22, 1917, Mother Cabrini died. She was buried at West Park, but her body was later moved to the chapel at the Mother Cabrini High School in New York.

Miracles that had seemingly attended Mother Cabrini from her birth—and were spoken about in whispers by many nuns in her order during her lifetime—persisted after her death. Several dramatic and miraculous cures, occurring after supplications to Mother Cabrini and attested to by physicians on the cases, as well as numerous other extraordinary events, caused the Vatican to waive the usual fifty-year period between the death of a candidate for sainthood and the start of the long and expensive Process that considers canonization by the Roman Catholic Church. In 1928, just eleven years after her death, Mother Cabrini's Cause was undertaken; ten years later she was declared *Tuto* in the ceremony of beatification. On July 7, 1946, Pope Pius XII conferred the office of Sainthood on Mother Cabrini. In the canonization rites at the Vatican Basilica, the Pope praised the new Saint Frances Xavier Cabrini: "Although her constitution was frail, her spirit was endowed with such singular strength that, knowing the will of God in her regard, she permitted nothing to impede her from accomplishing what seemed beyond the strength of a woman."

Thus the first United States citizen to become a saint was an immigrant from Italy. And although the existence of saints and the occurrence of miracles are often debated, everyone agrees that Mother Cabrini's work among a displaced and often despairing people was both miraculous and saintly.

The Maestro in America

Arturo Toscanini

"You must not conduct a piece of music until the notes have marched off the paper and come alive in your head and heart."

ONE OF THE most famous Italians to live in the United States never became a citizen, but we feel that he partly belonged to us because of his long residence here. At intervals throughout a half-century he conducted music in our opera and concert halls, on recordings, and over the radio, placing America in the forefront of the music world. His great gifts as well as the countless colorful anecdotes he engendered will be remembered for as long as his fame endures—which should be long indeed. If you ask somebody today to name the greatest orchestral leader of all time, the answer will doubtless be . . . Toscanini.

Arturo Toscanini was born in Parma on March 25, 1867. His father was a skilled tailor, but instead of providing properly for his wife, two daughters, and son, he preferred to sit reminiscing with his friends about the years he had served in Garibaldi's army. Arturo's mother was the family's firm backbone; a fiercely proud woman, she told her children never to show hunger—and once spanked Arturo soundly for eating a plateful of sausages at somebody else's house. Even in his affluent years Arturo Toscanini kept the spare diet of his childhood: a bowl of minestrone soup, a few bread sticks, a glass of red wine.

Toscanini's fond early memories were of evenings at home when family friends would drop by to play and sing tunes from popular Italian operas. The townspeople loved music, and Parmesan audiences were among the most eager in all of Italy. But they were exacting too. If a singer or musician performed with skill and feeling, he was showered with bravos and flowers. But woe to him who misplaced a note: the wrath of the entire Parma Theatre would descend upon him in the form of overripe tomatoes, empty wine bottles, and loud insults.

Some biographers have suggested that Toscanini's notorious rages at rehearsals originated in his Parmesan upbringing. Others claim that Toscanini had abnormally sensitive hearing. A single violin string out of tune in an orchestra of a hundred instruments, undetectable by most mortals, would seem to rend Toscanini's very soul. And he would lash out at the boorish world that permitted such offenses by hurling his baton, ripping up a score, or howling a peasant's earthy invective at the offender.

"Conductors are born, not made," said Toscanini in the years when courses in conducting had become standard offerings in music schools. He felt that all the instruction in baton techniques and the intricacies of orchestral composition, all the experience in summoning music from other men's instruments were useless and absurd if the conductor himself did not have the right head and heart for music. Whatever the reasons for Toscanini's uncanny ability and towering temperament, the two were apparently inborn and inseparable.

In school, Arturo's teacher was amazed by his phenomenal memory. She invited him to her home and, enchanted with her piano, he begged her to give him lessons. She soon realized that his musical potential lay far beyond her scope and persuaded his parents to send the nine-year-old boy to the Royal School of Music. Attending on a full scholarship, for nine years Arturo lived in the monastic atmosphere at the Parma conservatory, absorbing everything that could be taught about music. At the school's request he specialized in playing the cello; he himself would have chosen the piano.

Arturo's remarkable memory and his intense interest in music earned him the nickname *Il Genietto*—the little genius—among the students. He organized small groups to play clandestine concerts, breaking the school's rules. He astounded his teachers by committing whole scores to memory, knowing not just his own part but the other instrumental parts as well: while reading a score, he could somehow "hear" the music—the whole and all its intricate parts.

At the age of eighteen Arturo Toscanini was graduated from the conservatory with highest honors. But he faced an uncertain future as a cellist; he was a talented instrumentalist, but hardly a virtuoso. The best he could hope for was a lifetime of precarious, seasonal employment in orchestras at the many opera houses throughout Italy.

An opera company leaving for a season in South America hired Toscanini as a cellist and assistant chorus master. Squabbles arose, and performances fared badly. In Rio de Janeiro the conductor, a Brazilian now on his home ground, noisily accused the Italian singers and musicians of conspiring against him and then resigned. On June 25, 1886, the stranded Italian company—owed a month's pay and without funds for passage back to Italy—was to perform *Aïda*. An unruly audience eager for a brawl awaited them. "Down with the Italians!" was their battle cry; first the assistant conductor was brayed away, then the chorus master. What could they do without a conductor? Suddenly a singer thought of the young cellist who showed, while coaching them, that he thoroughly knew one opera after another. Put Toscanini out on the podium! But Arturo declined; he had never really conducted before and did not even know what to do with a baton. But then the whole company frantically urged him to try; as their last hope, he finally agreed.

Dressed in a dark suit several sizes too large, the short, thin, darkly shockheaded young man entered the lions' den. The audience was stunned to see the beardless youth who had been sent out to brave their ire. In the silence, Toscanini's baton descended sharply to start the overture to *Aïda;* the musicians followed as he, without a glance at his score, led them through the music he knew so well. The orchestra played as it had never done before; the singers sang with a glory they did not know they possessed. After a few minutes the audience realized that the crisis had brought forth an incandescent talent and responded with its whole heart. The "boy" conductor saved his company and became the toast of Rio. Most important of all, Toscanini had discovered his true calling. He was not to be the player of a single instrument, but the musician who "played" a whole orchestra of instruments. As a conductor he would interpret composers' scores, set and maintain the proper moods and tempos, and exercise a mastery over performances by regarding no detail too small for his attention, no conception too abstruse or grandiose and no effect too difficult for him to achieve. From now on Toscanini would serve the muse of music by grasping and conjuring with a slim stick twenty inches long.

Yet on his return to Italy in the fall of 1886, Arturo was once more just a cellist looking for work. News of his South American triumph had reached Italy only faintly. But Toscanini was not neglected for long. A singer rehearsing Catalani's new opera *Edmea*, knowing that the composer was unhappy with the conductor, told Toscanini to come to Turin and arranged a meeting with Catalani. The composer heard Arturo play through the score, which he had not seen before; impressed with his musical intelligence and sensitivity, he asked him to take over the première. The two men became close friends, and after Catalani's untimely death, Toscanini, through the years, loyally performed his music. He even named his first daughter Wally after the heroine in Catalani's *La Wally*.

Following this Italian debut, Toscanini considered himself a professional conductor and returned only sporadically to his cello, when conducting jobs were unavailable. However, he sought a cellist's chair at La Scala in Milan so as to be present in February of 1887 at the world première of *Otello*, the first Verdi opera in the sixteen years since *Aïda*. Toscanini always revered Verdi as both composer and man.

For the next ten years the fledgling conductor traveled to cities and towns throughout Italy to conduct operas and an occasional symphonic concert. He endured conditions prevalent in provincial opera houses: shoddy productions, third-rate singers, indifferent musicians, insufficient rehearsal time, backstage feuding, obstreperous audiences, and the necessity of performing a large repertoire of operas, many of which were repugnant to Toscanini's increasingly critical taste. Yet everywhere he went, Toscanini worked indefatigably, driving others as he drove himself. His reputation as a demanding yet inspiring conductor spread, along with the stories of his wild temper, his extraordinary memory, his acute hearing, and a perfectionism never before encountered in music-making.

Toscanini began to place Wagner upon a pedestal next to Verdi, not with quite the same affection but with a profound admiration for the German's dynamic, giant-sized opera-dramas. And beneath the powerful cataracts of sound, he unerringly found the touching, human-tuned song that to him provided the basis for good music. He introduced Wagnerian operas to Italian audiences whether they liked them or not—and at first, vehemently, they did not. In 1895, he gave the first Italian performance of *Die Götterdämmerung*. He had not yet visited Bayreuth, the Wagnerian Mecca, nor had he even heard the music performed before; thus his conception came fresh from the printed score and—like so many of his performances—shattered previous conventions. Under Toscanini's persuasive baton the German operas began to be accepted, even liked, in Italy.

In 1897, when he was thirty years old, Toscanini married Carla de Martini, a banker's daughter. The following year his son Walter was born. His wife knew little of music and probably he preferred it that way. She made him a comfortable home, gave birth to four children (a second boy died in childhood), sheltered the Maestro from petty problems, handled many of his business affairs, and served as his valet at rehearsals and concerts. To Toscanini, Carla was all a wife should be. Yet feminine beauty attracted him, and tales were often told of his romantic conquests.

As marks of Toscanini's increasing prestige, at Turin he

conducted the world premieres of *La Bohème* and *I Pagliacci*. Then, in 1898, he became the artistic director of the Teatro alla Scala in Milan, Italy's foremost opera house—the highest honor possible for an Italian conductor. The revered La Scala, then 120 years old, had been closed for a year due to inept management. It needed a strong guiding hand to help it back on its feet and Toscanini immediately gave it new life.

The domain he claimed in the production of operas encompassed not just the music played and sung, but the sets, lighting, costumes, staging of crowd scenes, and nuances of dramatic portrayals. Maestro Toscanini demanded perfection of everybody. Sometimes he patiently cajoled to get the effect he wanted, or showed how some passage should be sung by singing it himself. At other times the hallowed hall resounded with his raucous voice cursing his musicians or abusing a singer. And all for the sake of what he loved: music—not as it usually was, but as it should be.

Toscanini believed that the conductor's real job was to bring a composer's divinely inspired compositions to faithful fulfillment in performance. (Yet he lavished almost the same attention to lighter musical works as he did to the complex and profound.) Although he acted like a high priest serving an all-powerful muse, Toscanini really had an humble opinion of his role, considering it transitory and only second-handedly creative. "I am no genius," he insisted. "I have created nothing. I play the music of other men. I am just a musician."

At La Scala at the turn of the century Toscanini's artistry came into full flower—and consequently so did La Scala itself. There many of the world's finest singers got valuable training under Toscanini's strict but inspirational guidance. Tenor

Enrico Caruso's La Scala debut in *La Bohème* in 1900 was the real start of his worldwide fame.

But the Maestro's imperious demands, dire threats, and coarse insults wilted and rankled singers, musicians, and the business management. La Scala audiences were annoyed by his refusal to allow encores of favorite arias, which would break the moods he had worked so hard to create. From 1902 to 1905 Toscanini stayed away. When he returned to La Scala in the fall of 1906, he found discipline lax but both opera company and audiences more receptive to his reign. Yet Toscanini was tired of the everlasting, seemingly insoluble feuds. In 1908, both Toscanini and the La Scala manager, Giulio Gatti-Casazza, accepted offers from New York City's Metropolitan Opera Company. They would join in America such famed compatriots as Caruso and Antonio Scotti.

The Italian singers had already established Toscanini's fame on the other side of the Atlantic by high praise and tales of his fabulous eccentricities. When Toscanini finally touched American soil, reporters eagerly and noisily badgered him, but the Maestro simply looked unhappy and refused to answer their questions. *"Non so"*—I don't know—became his standard reply to everything. A photographer might snap a picture of the dapper Maestro, but if a flashbulb was ever used, Toscanini (whose eyes were hypersensitive to bright light) or some irate protector would rush at the offender, thrusting out fists and thundering abuse.

Toscanini's first performance at the Metropolitan Opera House came on November 16, 1908, with *Aïda*. Since it was the season's opening night, and one of the city's main social events, some of the Met's brightest stars performed too: Caruso, Scotti, Emmy Destin, Louise Homer. It set a style for the following years, when the gala opening night offered operas with the unmatchable Toscanini-Caruso combination.

Music critics hailed Toscanini's arrival as a comet in their midst. He was called "a strenuous force, a dominating power, a man of potent authority." And it was hoped that he would revive the popularity of the Italian lyric opera, eclipsed through years of German-dominated management and conducting at the Met. The partnership of Toscanini and Gatti-Casazza swiftly made up for the previous deficiency in Italian operas. During Toscanini's seven years at the Metropolitan, he prepared some eighty-five operas—and fifty-nine of them were Italian. But more importantly, he gave the opera house a firm discipline and inspirational musical direction which it had never known before. Afterwards, the Toscanini years would be regarded nostalgically as the Met's golden era. Gatti-Casazza remained at the Metropolitan for twenty-seven years, and to him goes much of the credit for putting the opera house on a sound financial basis while maintaining high artistic standards.

Meanwhile, of course, Toscanini was creating a new group of admirers and some American anecdotes. There was his fantastic memory that knew every instrument's part, every singer's role, and helped him immeasurably as his near-sightedness increased. With musicians, singers, and opera-house personnel he could be as demanding and ill-tempered as ever. No person was allowed to stray from Toscanini's precisely stated musical boundaries. One night the amiable Caruso, enchanted with a high note he had achieved, kept holding it. Finally the famous tenor stopped; and the impatient Toscanini shouted to him across the pit, "Have you finished, Caruso?" Nor did the Maestro grant prima donnas any special privileges. One of them, trying to dictate an aria's rhythm, said: "Maestro, you must conduct as I sing, for I am a star." Toscanini snapped back: "Signorina, the stars are in heaven. Here we are all artists, good or bad, and you are a bad artist."

One day several musicians complained to Gatti about the Maestro's terrible insults. Sympathetically, the Italian manager listened to samples of Toscanini's invective, then shrugged and said, "Ah, gentlemen, you should hear what he calls *me!*" Most dedicated musicians learned to endure Toscanini's explosive and tyrannical temperament, realizing that his dire insults were not given personally but awarded artistically. They came from a man haunted by a perfectionism that was total and relentless; a tiny musical error could wound the Maestro at the very core of his being. And just as he railed at them, he abused himself: *"Stupido* Toscanini!" Beseeching his orchestra, he would cry out instructions: "Weep, in the name of God!" And, always, *"Canta"*—sing!— for from their instruments he wanted the beauty of song. They marveled at the humanly expressive sounds he miraculously drew from their instruments. Much of the time Toscanini "sang along" with the orchestra, emitting an eery, high-pitched sound a musician described as the wail of a disembodied banshee. Yet he seemed utterly unaware of his compulsive crooning. Sometimes he stopped his orchestra and demanded to know, *"Who* is making that noise?"

At the Metropolitan Opera, Toscanini re-established the popularity of Italian operas. And under his baton came the world première of Puccini's *The Girl of the Golden West,* the American première of *Boris Godunov* with the Russian basso Feodor Chaliapin, and performances of most of Wagner's operas, which always gave the Maestro his most challenging yet taxing work. In 1910, the Metropolitan Opera

Company, with Toscanini, made an unprecedented visit to Europe.

In New York the Maestro avoided "society," confining his social life to family and intimate friends—most of them musicians. A demonic tyrant at rehearsals, during public performances Toscanini was actually shy. An audience's warm response to his conducting baffled and upset him. "What do they want me to do?" he would ask, bewildered, when applause grew clamorous. He felt that music should be a means of spiritual communion; opera houses and concert halls were sacred temples. When music—whether played by his own orchestra or somebody else's—approached the perfection he sought in it, he wept unashamedly: "It is so beautiful, I cannot help it."

If an ardent admirer placed a floral wreath at the Maestro's feet as he made his final bow, an unpardonable sin was committed. "Flowers are for prima donnas and corpses," Toscanini declared, "and I am neither." Blanching with insult and fury, Toscanini then might rush off to his dressing room, from which nothing or nobody could budge him until his rage had worn itself out. Or else he would swiftly depart from the opera house on foot; hatless, coatless, oblivious to rain or snow, to traffic or crowds milling along Broadway, he plunged toward the haven of his hotel apartment.

Toscanini grew dissatisfied with the Metropolitan Opera Company just as he had with La Scala. He had never liked its repertory system, which rotated productions in performance rather than giving a single opera for as long as attendance merited; the repertory plan made a tangle of rehearsals, performances, and artists' schedules that defied satisfactory solutions. Then too, he always insisted on the best, regardless of price, and Gatti-Casazza tried to balance the Met's budget by paring down costs and giving popular operas guaranteed to fill the large house nightly during the first uneasy months of World War I.

In the spring of 1915, without saying farewells or displaying any intention to return, the Maestro left for Italy. There his son Walter was in the army; he himself wanted to assist the Italian war effort. Toscanini gave a number of benefit concerts and even traveled to the front, sometimes to conduct bands under bombardment. But despite his patriotism, he angered Italian chauvinists objecting to programs that contained music by Haydn, Mozart, Brahms, Beethoven, and Wagner. Although they were Germans, Toscanini said, their music was written for all mankind; so he continued to perform their immortal works.

During the war years, Toscanini's family lived off his savings. After the Armistice, equally disenchanted with war and the music world's impresarios, Toscanini entered politics for his first and only time; he ran for a deputy post on the Socialist ticket. But he and a fellow aspirant named Benito Mussolini both lost. When the management of La Scala begged him to return, to supervise the remodeling of the opera house and the reorganization of the opera company, Toscanini responded. For the eight seasons of this second period as artistic director of La Scala, Toscanini was its absolute ruler.

While he reigned at La Scala, a far more dangerous dictator ruled Italy after 1922, when Mussolini and his Blackshirts seized control of the government. All concert halls and opera houses were required to decorate their lobby walls with pictures of Il Duce; Toscanini refused to have them at La Scala. Recognizing Toscanini's great national popularity, the Fascists long avoided an open conflict with him. Yet he bluntly denounced them and their leader wherever he went, privately and publicly: "We must have truth and freedom of speech at any price, even if that price be death. I have said to our Fascisti time and time again, 'You can kill me if you wish, but as long as I am living I shall say what I think.' " Before any public performance the two Italian anthems—the Royal March and the Fascist *Giovinezza*—had to be played. Toscanini wanted no part of this foolishness: "La Scala is not a beer garden or Fascist propaganda territory." So when an important musical affair absolutely demanded the playing of the martial songs, a seedy street band was hired to march on stage and wheeze them out—while the Maestro stood by with his arms folded, looking thoroughly disgusted.

Endowed with an incredible amount of energy to devote to music—and perhaps having a sure instinct for survival—Toscanini returned to New York in 1926 to make his conducting debut with the New York Philharmonic. During the next few years he divided his time between Milan and New York, his New York commitment assuming greater importance when he became the Philharmonic's principal conductor. In 1929, he resigned his post at La Scala, bringing to an end the thirty-year period of opera-conducting, during which the world's finest singers faced his baton.

Once more Toscanini gave America his great gifts and his mercurial temperament. At Carnegie Hall, Toscanini proved a box-office wonder; nearly all his concerts were sell-outs through the years. The New York public eagerly bought seasons' tickets or queued up to obtain seats for any Toscanini performance. They listened, transfixed, to brilliantly interpreted Beethoven symphonies; to delicate Mozart concertos; to thundering Wagnerian overtures; to the mood music of the contemporary Italian composer Respighi. As his loyal attendants at these musical rites, audience members would feel properly scolded when, straggling in after the concert had begun, they would be told by the Maestro after halting his orchestra, "You are late!" Meanwhile, Toscanini became a household name throughout the United States, for many of his Philharmonic concerts were broadcast over the radio.

Toscanini was the Maestro with a capital "M"; an absolute monarch in the world of music, during the 1930s few critics or instrumentalists dared to quarrel with him. He set the fashion for conducting, and lesser men aped his style, his tempos, his conducting without a score, even his tirades—the latter producing discouraging results. "Nobody who had the honor of being browbeaten by the great Toscanini was going to put up with scoldings and tantrums on the part of any ordinary conductor," said Winthrop Sargeant, a musician-turned-critic.

Among his friends too Toscanini was the indisputable master, as described so fully by the music critic Samuel Chotzinoff in *Toscanini: An Intimate Portrait.* They loved him for his infectious gaiety, his childlike simplicity, his mischievous pranks, his enthusiasms, his intensely human warmth. They endured his black moods, his perpetual private and professional feuds, his petulant opinions, his occasionally churlish behavior—and studied his frequent character transformations with utter fascination.

While Toscanini was the principal conductor of the New York Philharmonic, he also continued conducting abroad. His first major commitment was to the Bayreuth Festival, to which he had been invited in 1930. He was the first non-German deemed worthy to conduct opera at Wagner's exalted Festspielhaus. Toscanini's presence came like a rude shock to Wagner-worshippers. Disregarding the way things were always done, he pored over Wagner's scores, perused his writing, and proved to detractors that his startling innovations actually fulfilled Wagner's original ideas. For two seasons Toscanini worked at Bayreuth, upsetting routines and gaining even wider fame.

Toscanini liked Bayreuth because of its intense and pure concentration upon music. But his paradise suddenly ended when the Nazis came to power. Hitler himself sent a letter to the Maestro, urging his return to Bayreuth, which was becoming a shrine for the minions of the Master Race, who grotesquely distorted Wagner's Teutonic myths for racist purposes. Revolted by the Nazis, Toscanini pointedly ignored Hitler's invitation and in the following summers he conducted at Salzburg just across the German border. Then came the German Anschluss of 1938—and Austria was no more. So the Maestro moved on to Lucerne, Paris, and Tel Aviv, always to protest, by his presence and his music, totalitarian states and racist hatreds.

Toscanini had ended his tenure with the New York Philharmonic in 1936, after ten seasons and a total of 450 concerts. On April 29, in a Beethoven-Wagner program, he gave his farewell concert at Carnegie Hall. Thousands of his admirers were turned away from the box office. The Maestro said he would probably never return again from his homeland. President Roosevelt wrote a letter of regret, thanking him for "all that you have done for music during your stay among us." Toscanini, deeply touched, replied: "I shall never forget with what kindness and true understanding I have been received by the American people."

But Toscanini's residence in Italy could not last long. He had vowed never to conduct again there until the Fascists were defeated. While staying at his house on Via Durini in Milan or at his villa on an island in Lake Maggiore, Toscanini was constantly under police surveillance. Several times his passport was taken away, then returned because of pressure from influential friends.

In 1937, a year after his leaving America, as Toscanini was brooding about his future, he was offered a lucrative contract with the National Broadcasting Company and its affiliated recording company, RCA Victor. NBC wanted to create a special orchestra of virtuoso musicians for the Maestro and broadcast their concerts; RCA Victor would record their music in a specially constructed sound studio in Rockefeller Center. To everyone's surprise—for the Maestro had been firmly determined not to return to America—Toscanini accepted the proposition. He like the challenge of a "fresh" orchestra; and in America, where there was still peace, he could still work. Then seventy years old, at which age most ordinary mortals have retired from their lifetime careers, Toscanini was eager to start again; he seemed tireless, ageless.

Samuel Antek, a violinist with the NBC Symphony, recaptured those remarkable years with the elderly Maestro in *This Was Toscanini*. "Playing with him was like a musical and spiritual regeneration," said Antek. "Toscanini, like great leaders in other fields, had the gift of sweeping away the cobwebs of lost faiths, of dulled sensitivities. . . . Music-making became once more a hallowed calling and you felt musically reborn."

For sixteen years the "Old Man," as his orchestra fondly dubbed him, gave those musicians—and through them, the world—the last full measure of his musical artistry: the intense joy and the seering pain that music had always held for him. Age scarcely diminished his ardor, his memory, his definite opinions, his perpetual pursuit of the ever-elusive perfecting of a symphony, a passage, even a single note. "Play with your hearts, not your instruments," he commanded. With the mysterious power of a master sorcerer, Toscanini seemed to call upon the very souls of his musicians to follow him.

With him, conducting was not a mechanical act of holding a baton to beat time like a metronome and signal the entry of orchestral sections, or the arm-flailing, torso-gyrating, head-rolling display of a podium show-off. Toscanini was spare and conservative in his gestures. Making his kind of music meant summoning forth into life from an orchestra of men the wonderful sounds he heard as he studied a score. "You must not conduct a piece of music until the notes have marched off the paper and come alive in your head and heart," he advised a young conductor friend.

But if Toscanini's gentle persuasion failed, inevitably the air was rent by the Maestro's curses. (For a hapless fellow countryman he reserved a terrible affront: "I cannot believe you are an Italian!") And if his rage required physical expression, he might fling down his watch and grind it underfoot. (After one such episode the NBC staff began to provide him with one-dollar watches inscribed, "For rehearsals only.") He could snap his baton in half or throw it at somebody. (He was sued at least once by an injured musician.) He would tear his score to shreds, upset his music stand and kick it soundly; or take off his jacket and rend it at the seams. Afterwards, he usually got the results he wanted. For weeks Toscanini might amble along amiably, without a tantrum, with scarcely a frown. And his men would worry. Was something wrong with their "Old Man"? Was he losing his fire? Then suddenly some misdeed would bring out the Maestro's fury in all its famous splendor. The chastened men felt re-assured and relieved: Toscanini was still in good form; obviously there was nothing to fret about.

In 1940, the NBC Symphony made a long tour of South America, where the Maestro endeared himself to his musicians through his constant interest in their comfort and welfare. Toscanini lived at Villa Paulina, the home he had bought in Riverdale, outside of Manhattan. When the United States entered the Second World War, Toscanini followed events with unflagging interest and concern. Although friends urged him to become an American citizen, he declined, not wishing to desert the other anti-Fascists exiled with him in America. The NBC Symphony gave frequent charity performances during the war, and the Maestro even permitted a film to be made of his performance of Verdi's "Hymn of the Nations." In early 1945, as Toscanini was starting a concert of all-Italian music, he heard of Mussolini's death. "Good," he said. "Now we must play well."

Toscanini refused to return to Italy until the Fascist-propped king, Victor Emmanuel III, left the throne and a democratic rule was established. He had given a million lire for the restoration of La Scala, nearly destroyed in the bombardment of Milan. In April of 1946, Toscanini saw his homeland again, and on May 11 he conducted the first concert in the rebuilt La Scala. Everywhere he went, Toscanini was hailed as a champion of freedom. The new president conferred upon him an honorary life senatorship. The Maestro, however, refused it because he wished to stay out of politics and thereby offended some Italians, who thought that he no longer loved his country. But although Toscanini made most of his music now in America, his heart had hardly left Italy. In the post war years he spent the concert season months in New York and took long summer vacations at his old home in Milan.

Toscanini had made his first recording in 1921, when he visited the United States with the orchestra from La Scala. In the 1930s he had often recorded with the New York Philharmonic. Through his years with the NBC Symphony he worked sedulously with RCA Victor technicians to record many of his notable performances. It was grueling labor for him—work that gave little satisfaction, since he believed that the recording process distorted his music. (In recent years musicologists agree with his opinion, placing most of the blame on a peculiar resonance in the recording studio.) Whatever the technical defects discernible by experts, these records provide an enduring collection of Toscanini's interpretations—impossible to have had before the age of electronics.

In March of 1948, in an all-Wagner program, Toscanini made his first television appearance; millions of Americans now saw him conduct for the first time, although for years his concerts broadcast on the radio had resounded in their homes. In 1950, the Maestro, eighty-three years old, undertook a six-week tour of twenty American cities with his orchestra, traveling in a special train with a dozen pullman cars. Usually at his best form during rehearsals, tending to "freeze up" at public concerts, Toscanini was now relaxed and very pleased to have so many musically sophisticated audiences.

The "Old Man" seemed indestructible and immortal. On his eightieth birthday Toscanini had received from his orchestra a clock that would not have to be wound for a half-century. "Just think," he told them, "in fifty years everybody here will be dead—everybody but me." Yet in 1951 Toscanini's legs began to trouble him, and a guard rail was placed around the podium. But he refused to sit down while conducting. "As long as I am here," he growled, "I stand and conduct. I don't sleep!" Later in the year he mourned his wife's death so deeply that he seemed to have abandoned music forever. But music to Toscanini was life itself, so after a few months he again took up his baton. For several more years, as his health slowly declined, he continued to serve his muse.

In the spring of 1954, NBC officials decided to disband the Symphony. They considered Toscanini's condition too precarious; also for some time the orchestra had operated at a deficit. Before the NBC Symphony's demise was made public, its eighty-seven-year-old conductor reluctantly and sadly submitted his resignation from his last post. Toscanini's final concert was given at Carnegie Hall on April 4. He launched vigorously into the Wagner program; but then, in the midst of orchestral music from *Tannhäuser,* his baton faltered. He passed a hand over his eyes and looked stunned: his fantastic memory had fled. For several bars the orchestra went on without him and finally halted. After a few miserable and confusing moments, Toscanini collected himself and resumed his time-beating—yet still in almost a daze. The rest of the concert was given without further embarrassment. At its conclusion Toscanini stepped down from the podium and was escorted offstage; he did not return to take a bow. It made a melancholy, indelible finish to a conducting career of sixty-eight years.

For a few more weeks the Maestro and his orchestra continued working together, finishing up some recordings. Then he left for Italy. His musicians remained together, calling their new orchestra the Symphony of the Air. Their first concert was given as a tribute to him; they played without a conductor—in front of them a dramatically empty podium.

Toscanini lived for a while in Milan, but then returned to Riverdale, where his son Walter, for years his manager, was supervising at Villa Paulina the massive job of "cleaning up" and reissuing several decades of Toscanini recordings. Feeble, almost blind, Toscanini now listened raptly to the music of his long lifetime, as so many phrases and passages evoked strong memories and feelings; quite unconsciously, his hands followed the music, setting the tempo, bringing in the second violins, summoning a soprano. The world beyond his own room had faded away; only the glorious music of his past now remained.

The great Maestro died at Villa Paulina in Riverdale on January 16, 1957, at the age of eighty-nine. After a funeral Mass at St. Patrick's Cathedral in New York, his body was returned to a final rest in Italy. But much of what Toscanini was, in spirit, remained in America, where he had lived off and on through a half-century and conducted three major orchestras. In the United States too, the music that Toscanini had made was captured on the black plastic discs and slender tapes that generations after him could listen to—and know something of the incomparable magic that was Toscanini's.

A Banker for Americans

A. P. Giannini

"Our conception of a bank is that of a great public servant—an institution run in the interest and for the welfare of the people it serves."

THE LARGEST privately owned bank in the world today was started in California by the son of Italian immigrants. With fifteen billion dollars in resources, more than seven and a half million depositors, 28,500 employees, and over 900 domestic and overseas branches, the Bank of America owes its success to the foresight, daring methods, and energy of its founder. A. P. Giannini was a rugged American individualist with an Italian stamp; yet the financial empire he built from the ground up, unlike those of other captains of industry, was not for himself or his descendants but for the people at large.

Attracted to the warm and fertile Santa Clara Valley in California, Luigi and Virginia Giannini emigrated from Genoa in 1869. Luigi came from a long line of vineyardists; he loved land and its produce—a deep attachment passed on to his first son. Amadeo Peter Giannini was born on May 6,

1870, in San Jose, where his parents ran a small hotel. They were soon able to make a down-payment on a forty-acre ranch near Alviso, the port town on south San Francisco Bay that shipped the Valley's many crops to San Francisco. Life went well for them; their orchard and garden gave abundant yields and two more sons, Attilio and George, were born. Then in 1877, in front of young Amadeo's own eyes, Luigi Giannini was killed by a crazed neighbor in an argument over a one-dollar debt.

Virginia Giannini continued to farm her land and rear her three sons. She got to know Lorenzo Scatena, a young man from Lucca, whose horse and cart carried her fruits and vegetables to Alviso. Firm, but gentle and good-humored, he surely would be a good father to her boys. A year after her husband's death, Mrs. Giannini married Scatena. The marriage was a good one. "Pop" was always loved by his three stepsons, who were as dear to him as the three children he and his wife had later. With Virginia's encouragement, Scatena left Alviso in 1881 to get a job in the produce-commission business in San Francisco. In the following year he started his own company and was on his way to acquiring a modest fortune.

"Pop" Scatena's enterprise attracted young Amadeo. The boy excelled in school, but liked even better the smells and sights, the noisily competitive scene, around Washington Street, where daily at dawn boats arrived loaded with produce from the rich California farmlands. At the wharves, Scatena bought up large quantities of perishable fruits and vegetables and resold them later in the morning to retail merchants. To be successful, a produce-commission dealer had to be quick-thinking, shrewd but honest, and willing to take risks. He also had to have strong fists.

Although his mother had lofty plans for his future, Amadeo followed in his stepfather's footsteps. Mrs. Scatena finally bowed to the inevitable and sent her eldest son to business school for a half-year. Then he began to work full-time for "Pop."

At the age of fifteen A. P. Giannini was already man-sized—six feet tall and weighing 170 pounds; and he had a deep, powerful voice. On Washington Street he quickly became known and respected. Soon he was taking buying trips among growers and shippers throughout California. Tireless, trustworthy, and thorough, he made many business friends; bold and enterprising, he constantly developed new ways to improve business and expand L. Scatena and Company far beyond its original scope. When A. P. was nineteen, "Pop" gratefully gave him a third share of the business; two years later—by now a giant of a man—A. P. became a full partner. During the next ten years he founded his first empire: the largest produce-commission house on the Pacific Coast.

Although Giannini always concentrated with singleminded force on pursuing business goals, he had some spare time for diversions, which in his early manhood included music, politics, baseball, theatre—and romance. Tall, dark, and handsome, the well-heeled Amadeo got many a sigh from young ladies in North Beach—the San Francisco section close to the wharves, where the large Italian population lived and worked.

In his early twenties, A. P. met Clorinda Agnes Cuneo; thereafter no other woman drew his eye. What did it matter if she was engaged to a young doctor studying abroad? The Giannini style—enthusiasm coupled with a dogged refusal to accept a "no" on anything he really wanted—was already well-established in business. Now his vitality, persistence,

and genial aura of success operated as well in romance. The
lady's gentle refusals finally were changed to a happy "yes."
In September of 1892, she and A. P. were married. The
Gianninis lived at first in San Francisco; later they moved to
San Mateo, seventeen miles southward, and built Seven Oaks,
their comfortable home throughout their long marriage. In
1894, their first child, Lawrence Mario, was born; after him
came Virgil and Claire.

Becoming a millionaire or merely hoarding money were
never goals for Giannini. Success at his work motivated him
instead. "The making or saving of money represents only
by-products of one's work," he maintained. "The important
thing is that any young man should work hard at whatever
interests him most." A. P. was fascinated with the process of
acquiring money just to be able to watch it work. Money was
powerful: it could create something that had never been
there before—a building, a business, a job, an opportunity.
For him, money had a human scale and meaning; it did not
interest him unless it was connected with other people.

Giannini relished challenges and obstacles. Having built
a large and secure enterprise, at the age of thirty-one he
retired from business. He sold his half-share in L. Scatena and
Company to other employees and announced that he would
now devote his time to managing various real-estate holdings.
When his wealthy father-in-law died, A. P. was appointed
administrator of an estate that consisted of scattered proper-
ties. A. P. judiciously tended it, distributing the income
among the eleven heirs on the sensible basis of need.

Part of his wife's legacy were shares in the Columbus
Savings and Loan Society, a bank created by prosperous
Italian-Americans as a safe repository for their money. After
Giannini took over a directorship in the Society, he began to

express some novel ideas. Money should not be piled up in vaults or kept bound in sterile paper securities; it should be lent out to work for people who needed it. San Francisco, the "money center" of the West, had many banks, but they were only interested in big people with big money, not in immigrants with dreams and hard-working hands. All around were thrifty and industrious Italians who, with a little assistance from a bank, could start a barber shop or restaurant, buy a fishing boat or a small farm, build a hotel or just homes for their families.

A. P. Giannini urged his fellow bank directors to take a chance on the "little fellow" and lend him money at a reasonable interest rate—6 per cent instead of the 10 or 12 per cent that the "loan sharks" charged. A small loan secured on real estate or even on a man's acknowledged good character would enable him to launch some enterprise that could expand, thus increasing the bank's business with him, to both their advantages. Good will could further be advanced by lending money for financial emergencies in businesses or families and by carrying mortgages on homes. And, A. P. asked, what about all the cash hidden unproductively at home—in jars at the back of kitchen shelves or tucked under mattresses, saved by provident yet timid people who had never been welcomed into banks? Their money would not only be far safer in a bank but could earn them a small but steady interest of $3\frac{1}{2}$ per cent for remaining in circulation while being used by other people.

Giannini's suggestions horrified most of the conservative bank directors. After months of trying to persuade them otherwise, A. P. resigned his directorship. "I'll start a bank of my own and run it according to the principles you refuse to adopt," he told them. A few other directors liked his ideas and left with him, willing to help start a bank that would serve "the little man who needs a little money."

A. P. Giannini first went to James J. Fagan, a shrewd banker friend who told him about the proper procedures in starting a new bank and aided him in working out legal details and preparing to sell stock to finance the bank's operating capital. Fagan bought shares in A. P.'s "baby bank" and was glad to serve as one of its directors; to make him feel at home with his ten fellow officers, all Italian-Americans, he was jovially called "Giacomo" (James). Giannini became vice-president of the new bank. His many business friends bought shares at $100 each, their holdings limited to a hundred shares. Meanwhile, A. P. walked around North Beach to talk people into buying a share or two, or a dozen if they could; he wanted everybody to feel that his bank did not belong to rich people. Known and trusted in the Italian settlement, Giannini soon had sold some $300,000 in shares. Confidently, he leased a building at the triangular corner where Columbus and Washington Avenues intersect. At the very apex was a saloon; A. P. remodeled it into a one-room bank and hired three full-time employees.

The Bank of Italy opened for business on October 17, 1904. Through its doors on that Monday walked the curious, the hopeful, and the thrifty who habitually hid their cash away at home. All came to see the bank that had been expressly created for them. At the door Giannini greeted each of them with a warm handshake, a question about the family's health, a word about the weather. No cold and reserved banker in the time-worn stereotype, he was a big, friendly man, always at his best among ordinary people. Whenever he heard of a new baby's arrival, he fetched a five-dollar gold piece from his pocket and gave it to the proud parent, a generous gesture repeated over and over through the years; usually, of course, the pleased recipient took it right over to the counter and started a savings account in the newcomer's name. A. P.'s perceptive glance could spot a shy, would-be depositor who knew nothing of deposit slips and passbooks and perhaps could not even write; in a moment he turned the person over to a special assistant who courteously and simply explained the bank's role in handling money and helped fill out the forms. Everyone, whether rich or poor, was made to feel welcome at Giannini's bank.

On the first day, the Bank of Italy received $8,780 in twenty-eight new accounts. Within a month it was making loans at reasonable rates to business concerns; people whose needs merited small sums also got loans. Shocking stodgy bankers, the little Bank of Italy began to advertise its services in newspapers and on billboards. ("If business is worth having," A. P. explained, "it is worth going after.") Giannini did not want to have "just another foreign-colony bank." The Bank of Italy, he said, wanted "to do business with everybody and anybody who needed our help—regardless of nationality or place of business or newness or smallness." His "baby bank" soon grew out of its swaddling clothes and employed six people and even gave its hardworking vice-president a small salary. Within a year and a half after its start, the Bank of Italy's resources totalled nearly a million dollars. Then came a rude jolt.

At dawn on April 18, 1906, San Francisco was rocked by an earthquake that left incredible destruction and chaos. The temblor roused Giannini in San Mateo. He surveyed the slight damage done to his sturdy house; his next concern was for his little bank in the big city. Since trains could not run on the twisted and shattered tracks, he hitched rides and walked to

San Francisco, finding the Bank of Italy unharmed except for fallen plaster. It was even open for business.

Like many San Franciscans, in spite of the earthquake his clerks had reported for work that day. As they did every morning, they went to the vault at the Crocker National Bank to get the cash kept there at night, then opened up the bank. But reports of widespread looting and the spread of a hundred fires that could not be checked because of the failure in the water supply had made the clerks apprehensive. They were greatly relieved to see their boss.

Giannini at once locked the bank doors. He was certain that within hours the fire would consume his bank building. Borrowing two wagons from "Pop" Scatena's warehouse, he and his men filled them with the bank's possessions—including three canvas bags from the vault, containing $80,000 in cash. Over these he piled crates and sacks of produce, then left for a relative's house at the edge of town. There he and his clerks hastily dined, replaced the produce in the wagons by household furnishings, to make them look like refugee caravans, and set off for Giannini's house in San Mateo. Taking a slow, circuitous route, they arrived twelve hours later; A. P. hid the cash bags in the cinder box below a fireplace, harnessed his horse to a buggy, and left again for San Francisco.

Giannini found his bank a smoking mound of black rubble. But by comparison his loss was very small. In the great fire that lasted four days, some 28,000 buildings were burned and property worth $500 million was destroyed.

Even before the fire was over, A. P. Giannini was planning the rebuilding of his own bank and boldly plotting ways by which he could help to resurrect San Francisco. Thanks to his clerks' adherence to routine, he at least possessed ready cash; most other banks' cash lay in fireproof vaults too hot to open for several weeks. Giannini sent ship captains to the north to fill their holds with lumber for new buildings—for who would ever abandon San Francisco? He also asked other bankers to open their banks as soon as possible and, for the city's sake, lend leniently, so that the citizens could start all over again.

In a letter to his depositors Giannini said that he would advance money to any of them who wished to rebuild; withdrawals and loans would be given only for that purpose. The Bank of Italy would operate in two temporary locations: the office of his brother, Dr. Attilio Giannini, and on the wharf at the end of Washington Street, where the bank counter was a plank supported by two barrels.

A. P.'s energetic enthusiasm, stirred by the challenge of difficult months ahead, inspired others. With a firm confidence in his fellow citizens' abilities, Giannini fully exercised now his uncanny knack at judging the characters of people asking for loans. Often he was willing to take a chance on someone just because his calloused hands showed he could do hard work. Giannini stretched far the original $80,000 in cash, partly by acquiring many new savings accounts. Mainly due to his encouragement, North Beach, the Italian section of the city, recovered from the fire ahead of the others. And by the end of that disastrous year of 1906, A. P.'s bank had managed to double its business: its depositors numbered 2,644 and its assets were close to $2 million.

In the following year Giannini went to the East Coast. Studying banking conditions there, he was disturbed by what he saw. An economic depression had already hit Europe. And in America the craze for stock-investing had dangerously lowered banks' cash reserves. Back in San Francisco, A. P.

told "Giacomo" Fagan at the Crocker National that a financial panic would soon seize the nation; banks unable to supply cash to depositors demanding the return of their savings would be ruined. Although the more experienced Fagan laughed off the warning, Giannini began to prepare quietly for the crisis ahead. He built up a big surplus of cash at his bank by cutting down on lending, vigorously soliciting new accounts, and handing out paper currency instead of "hard" money.

In the fall of 1907, the panic that Giannini had predicted started in New York, then spread rapidly westward, reaching San Francisco by October. Banks' cash assets vanished within hours as depositors withdrew their money. But A. P. Giannini's Bank of Italy sat securely on a big pile of gold and silver. When a "run" started at Fagan's "big brother" bank, the Crocker National, A. P. went over to help out. In his booming voice he told the long lines of people waiting for money that the nearby Bank of Italy had plenty of cash and would be glad to honor their passbooks. The crowd, reassured, soon dispersed, and the Crocker was saved from acute embarrassment, if not actual disaster.

The Panic of 1907 convinced both national and state leaders that strong legislation was needed to prevent similar banking disturbances in the future. New ideas, like the Federal Reserve System, were developed. And old but neglected methods were suggested too: like the plan proposed in 1908 at a bankers' convention in Denver. Giannini was one of the few present who listened carefully to the speaker—Woodrow Wilson, then president of Princeton University. Wilson recognized the ordinary citizen's attitude toward banks: "The banks of this country are remote from the people and the people regard them as not belonging to them but as belonging to some power hostile to them." A. P. already understood that complaint well and was trying to remedy it. Wilson went on to suggest that a sturdy system of branch banks, simply and inexpensively run, could be created by large city banks to serve small communities that lacked big resources. He told the bankers to stop placing money in risky speculations. "There would be plenty of investments," he said, "if you carried your money to the people of the country at large. . . . Your money, moreover, would quicken and fertilize the country." Within a generation, Wilson predicted, the public's attitude toward banks and bankers could be radically changed.

This idea of "branch banking" excited A. P. Giannini. It had been tried by a few American banks in the past, but it had failed because of poor management. It had succeeded, however, on the Continent, in England, and in Canada. Why shouldn't it prosper in the United States too? Although the Bank of Italy hardly fitted Wilson's vision of branch banks established by banks with huge assets, A. P. felt he could start on a small scale, taking one step at a time. He already had a second bank office in San Francisco. He now visited Canada to study branch-banking methods; he came away with some concrete plans.

Giannini convinced his fellow bank directors that his approach was feasible. "By opening branches in different localities," he reasoned, "we will be able to diversify our business and thus be able to render better and broader service. Crops come on the market at different times in different sections. Growers in one district will be paying off loans at the time growers in another section will be needing funds. By building up a big central institution at headquarters, we will be able to engage much abler men than the little, independent, isolated banks can afford to employ, and the services of our experienced executives will be available for all our customers whether in San Francisco or in other places."

In 1909, the California state legislature passed an act to regulate banking within the state. It contained a clause that interested Giannini: branch-banking offices would be permitted to open if the state banking superintendent could "ascertain to his satisfaction that the public convenience and advantage will be promoted." For each new branch, a bank would have to add $24,000 to its capital. In three months Giannini made his first move into branch banking by acquiring a bank in San Jose. There, as he would do in so many towns in the future when his branches opened up, A. P. personally solicited accounts; he sold stocks in his bank to local citizens; he went into stores and factories and talked with farmers in their fields, getting to know intimately the products and problems of that area. (Later on, when his executives scolded him for working too hard out among the people, he would reply, "This is what I like—you can't call it work.")

The Bank of Italy made bigger strides all the time. In 1908, it had moved into a new building it had financed in the main financial district of San Francisco. Several city banks were taken over as branches as well as a bank in San Mateo. Then in 1913 Giannini moved southward to Los Angeles, the fastest growing area in the state, upsetting the local bankers, who feared this "Frisco" foreigner's invasion of their territory. PARK BANK TAKEN OVER BY ITALIANS, read one resentful headline. True to his past style, he ran newspaper ads in seven languages and put up eye-catching billboards: THE BANK FOR JUST PLAIN

FOLKS . . . and WOULD MONEY HELP YOU? "Bargain basement banking" one irate banker called it; "department store banking" was a kinder version. Giannini accepted the insults with equanimity, for he was a shrewd man with insight into the public's future needs and expectations. "The bank of tomorrow," he said, "is going to be a sort of department store, handling every service the people may want in the way of banking, investment, and trust service."

By 1914, as war engulfed Europe, Giannini's banking empire was poised to expand throughout the state. Warring nations abroad needed food, and California's agricultural lands began to supply it. The Bank of Italy started picking up banks in farm communities by the dozens. It usually took over faltering banks, thereby rescuing depositors from ruin. Usually too, the old bank's staff was retained, since they knew well the town and its people; they were then instructed in Bank of Italy's unique attitudes and innovations. And when the United States entered the war the Bank of Italy assisted in the purchase of lands and farming machinery and aided in the development of California's new industries.

As branch after branch was added to the network, A. P. himself shaped the role that Bank of Italy would take in any community throughout the state, even in the nation. "Our fundamental principles are woven into our structure," he said. "Our conception of a bank is that of a great public servant—an institution run in the interest and for the welfare of the people it serves." Departments of experts gave customers advice on agricultural and industrial problems. The Bank of Italy purchased local and state bonds for public works construction. Investments were made in the burgeoning movie industry in Hollywood. Auto loans were started. And even children were encouraged to start savings accounts; weekly, they brought nickels and dimes to school to give to a representative from Bank of Italy. The cost of handling these thousands of small accounts was high, but it paid off by gaining good will and future business. Fully 60 per cent of these savings accounts remained when the children grew up. ("Our best crop is always these young Americans," said A. P.)

As his bank's business multiplied by ever greater figures, so did Giannini's concern for his increasing personnel. He gave them liberal benefits and began a profit-sharing plan. Always expecting of others what he gave of himself in work capacity, dedication, and actual accomplishment, and known for an explosive temper if something was done badly or stupidly, A. P. might have been a terrible and tyrannical boss had he not also possessed a personable warmth, humor, simplicity, and genuine human interest in his employees. His own enthusiasm and energy infused everybody around him, both clerks and executives.

To Giannini's vast pride and pleasure, his elder son, Lawrence Mario—known as Mario to his family, "L. M." to bank people—was turning out to be his right-hand helper. Although Mario's health was precarious (he suffered from hemophilia), he worked as intensely as his father—and that was hard indeed. He was a "natural banker." A boy of ten when the Bank of Italy was established, he had grown up in a house where banking was the main topic of discussion. While going to college, he worked part-time in the bank; eventually he took a Doctor of Laws degree with special emphasis on the legal aspects of finance. Quite happily he worked his way through every department of the bank before he became an executive. On his own, L. M. suggested and developed some of the bank's highly successful innovations.

By 1921, both the Bank of Italy and Giannini were na-

tionally known. Having outgrown its quarters, the bank
moved to a new location: the second largest bank building
in the nation. The strength of branch banking was proven
that same year when the Bank of Italy experienced its first
"run." When its branch in Santa Rosa, falsely rumored to be
in trouble, was jammed with hysterical depositors demanding
their money back, a million and a half dollars in cash, a
third of it in gold, was sent immediately from San Francisco.
The people went home, convinced that the big Bank of Italy
had plenty of hard cash. (A small "unit" bank would surely
have expired during such a "run.") A decade later, when a
Sacramento branch underwent a "run," Giannini sent bags
of money by plane and got there himself to help dispense it.
When the crisis was halted, reporters asked A. P. for his com-
ment. "Money talks," he said simply—making headlines
across the nation.

Giannini's success, however, disturbed a number of people: the town bankers who disliked his intrusions; other
ambitious city bankers; state and national officials who feared
the creation of a monopoly with a confusing array of assets.
Then too, stories were told of the Bank of Italy's supposed
heartlessness in foreclosing ranches whose owners had been
unable to make mortgage payments. During the lean years of
the 1920s, when overproduction had resulted in low produce
prices, the Bank of Italy had to take over many farms; but as
long as a farmer worked hard, he was allowed to remain as
a tenant, until either his luck or prices improved and he
could buy back his ranch.

Meanwhile, almost ceaselessly, both the California Banking Department and the Federal Reserve Board attempted to
stop the Bank of Italy's growth—partly to allow its com-
petitors, who resented the Italian banker's success, to gain

on him. Giannini's fighting spirit was roused. "If my op-
ponents hadn't forced me to it, time after time," he admitted,
"there would have been no driving, sustained efforts to top
the field." He employed skillful lawyers to steer the bank's
expansion within legal limits. By forming Bancitaly, a holding company with stockholders mainly in California, Giannini bought up many new banks and created several other
branch-banking systems that kept their original names until
1927, when he was finally permitted to consolidate them into
one large network. Called The Bank of Italy National Trust
and Savings Association, it had 276 branches, more than
4,000 employees, and over a million depositors. In just
twenty-two years Giannini's "baby bank" had grown into
the third largest bank in the United States.

Giannini's ambitious plans encompassed not only state-
wide banking, but the entire national as well. Through
Bancitaly, across the country, he bought up banks or sizable
shares in banks, laying a foundation for a time when, hopefully, federal law would permit branch banking across state
borders. And in a farther future, there was the whole world
to consider: A. P. began acquiring controlling interests in
foreign banks, notably a chain of banks in Italy.

A. P. Giannini's great reputation as a financier had caused
many Americans to leap onto his band wagon and invest in
stocks of Bank of Italy and Bancitaly. By the mid-1920s, A. P.
was much concerned over this eager speculation in his stocks,
which to him seemed dangerously overpriced. He warned
stockholders not to buy "on margin"—paying just 10 per cent
down to brokers. While vacationing in Europe early in 1928,
he learned that his fears had been apt. His two corporations
were suddenly hit by selling waves, and their stock values
plunged downward as panicky shareholders unloaded. The

Gianninis, father and son, probably poured some sixty million dollars into their failing stocks; they managed to save the two companies from extinction and to retain their loyal stockholders' savings.

To discourage further speculation, the Gianninis removed Bank of Italy and Bancitaly stocks from direct contact with the fluctuating stock exchange by creating a gigantic holding company. The Transamerica Corporation—TA for short— was to be the Giannini empire's only representative on the stock market. In its control would be Bank of Italy, Bancitaly, and numerous other bank stocks, plus major investments in a wide variety of business, insurance, and industrial companies in the country.

Wanting an experienced executive for TA from the New York world of finance, Giannini chose Elisha Walker, president of an investment house on Wall Street. Many of the Wall Street money-men clearly resented the entrance into their midst of the large, deep-voiced, direct-talking, superbly successful banker from the West Coast. ("We simply cannot have at the head of this nation's banking this Sicilian fruit vendor," complained one finical fellow.) Moreover, while acquiring his New York connections, Giannini had refused to submit to the all-powerful J. P. Morgan's dictates, thus incurring the terrible enmity of his investment-banking kingdom.

Transamerica Corporation proceeded on a whirlwind course of buying up still more controlling shares of banks and companies. Up soared the price of TA's stocks . . . until that disastrous October of 1929, when the great Wall Street balloon—inflated by a million dreams of winning wealth simply by buying and selling pieces of paper that represented shares in American businesses—finally burst and came crashing down. A nation obsessed by the desire to make magic money was now Depression-bound.

At first, Transamerica Corporation weathered the sharp decline in values. A. P. Giannini felt sure the situation would level off. Ailing, he left for a rest in Europe, leaving his empire to his trusted executives. Elisha Walker became TA's chairman of the board. Almost as soon as Giannini departed, TA ran into real difficulties. Its stock value took another bad fall, and soon frantic shareholders were selling at any price. L. M. Giannini kept his father informed of the happenings; he also told him he was beginning to distrust the attitudes and actions of Walker and other executives.

In September of 1930, A. P. returned briefly to California to survey the situation and participate in the official changing of the name of his bank—to Bank of America National Trust and Savings Association. The bank that had started in a re-modeled saloon and had catered to the Italians of San Francisco claimed resources of more than a billion dollars and had proved itself a bank for all Americans. Giannini's pride in his bank, however, was offset by worries over its future. In sorrow he saw for himself now that some of his most trusted officers had switched their loyalties to Walker.

Stricken with painful polyneuritis, Giannini lay gravely ill in an Austrian hospital as increasingly ominous news came daily from Mario. Walker was not handling the crisis in TA properly, he said. Walker's solution was to liquidate, to sell outright at distress prices, most of Giannini's prized assets: among them the carefully bought network of banks across the nation, acquired for a nationwide banking system—and the Bank of America. No Giannini could ever countenance such cowardice or submission, possibly even deceit. Resigning the TA presidency the better to fight

Walker's decision, L. M. made plans for regaining Giannini control of the corporation.

A. P. first fought to recover his health enough to leave the hospital and return home. By now he was convinced that Wall Street conspirators had enlisted Elisha Walker's assistance in destroying him. (It may never be known whether Giannini's interpretation was correct; but whatever the cause of the financial trouble, he had every right to dispute the dismembering by other hands of the great enterprise he had painstakingly built up through the years.)

A. P. had always enjoyed a good fight. Now the sick and aging man had the fight of his life before him. Doctors were amazed to see him struggling back to his feet so he could rejoin Mario and try to save his empire—most of all, his beloved bank. The ensuing proxy war would fully restore his lost health. A noisy and fierce contest against ruthless, skilled adversaries was apparently just the antidote the old fighter needed.

As soon as he could, A. P. sailed homeward, traveling under an assumed name so that nobody would learn of his return. He and Mario met in Canada for secret planning. In September of 1931, the news leaked out: Giannini had come back to battle for control of TA and Bank of America.

Now the battle of the "blues" and "whites" started among the thousands of TA stockholders, many of whom lived in California. A blue proxy meant a vote for Walker, a white one for Giannini. In the weeks leading up to the directors' meeting in February of 1932, when the proxies would be counted, A. P. and L. M. Giannini, with crews of helpers, traveled the length and breadth of California to gain support. They talked to TA shareholders anywhere they could gather a crowd, and tried to persuade them that the best way to regain the value of their stocks was to return A. P. to the control of the corporation which he had created and was now unwilling to abandon to Wall Street predators. "Throw the rascals out, and let honest, red-blooded California boys put their shoulders to the wheel!" Giannini cried. He showed that when he gave up the chairmanship of TA the stock was selling at 46½; now, with Walker running TA, the price was 4 and still falling. A. P. had operated TA for $300,000 a year; under Walker, expenses soared to $3 million. When A. P. was accused of taking a great deal of money from TA and Bank of America, it was shown that he had really plowed most of it back into the companies. Furthermore, a large chunk of profits due him—some million and a half dollars— he had given to the University of California to start a foundation specializing in agricultural research, a concrete way of assisting his state's development. Yet what had Walker done with his $100,000 salary?

For funds the Gianninis relied wholly on contributions; A. P. himself gave $50,000 borrowed on his life insurance. All "white" workers served without pay. On the other hand, Walker simply took money from the near-exhausted TA treasury to pay for his efforts to retain control. In the heat of frantic battle he and his cohorts employed many proxy solicitors, forbade Bank of America employees from assisting their old boss in any way under penalty of dismissal, and even required those owning TA shares to fill out blue proxies and to go out and actively get votes for Walker.

On February 15, 1932, when the proxies were counted at TA's head office in Wilmington, Delaware, A. P. had won by an overwhelming majority of votes; the "whites" outnumbered the "blues" by almost three to one. At the meeting a triumphant, newly vigorous Giannini was reinstated as the chairman of TA. Admiring reporters cheered him as "The Lochinvar who came out of the West," for he was the only man besides Henry Ford who had ever won a proxy battle with Wall Street financiers.

But Giannini had no time for or interest in gloating over his victory. Plans for putting his business back on its feet were instituted immediately. He was willing to overlook the part that bank workers had taken in following their superiors' commands. But a good hater when he had to be, A. P. ousted the once-trusted executives who had sided with Walker. Paring down all expenses, soliciting new accounts, and urging everybody to work extra-hard, Giannini imbued a confident spirit to all around him. Forty-one days after he took over, the decline in deposits at the Bank of America was halted; from then on, business was on the upswing.

As Giannini nursed Bank of America back to health, he was also helping to return California to prosperity from the Depression that engulfed the country. The bank bought state and city bonds which would provide widespread employment and assist in economic recovery; the most notable purchase was one for $6 million that launched work on the Golden Gate Bridge—a bond which citizens themselves had declined to support. A. P. started a "Back to Good Times" program that put up billboards all over the state urging people to "Keep Your Dollars Moving." "Depressions are the products of fear," he said—in line with Franklin D. Roosevelt's famous phrase, "We have nothing to fear but fear itself." Knowing that the nation needed a bold, imaginative leadership, Giannini supported FDR's candidacy. Roosevelt later gave a tribute in return: "In my opinion A. P. Giannini has done more to build California through his great bank and his personal efforts than any other Californian."

Banks everywhere were in peril. After Roosevelt's inauguration in March of 1933, he declared a bank holiday for some days while the Emergency Banking Act was pushed through Congress, to enable the federal government to gain closer control over banks. Meanwhile, officials of the Treasury Department went over the records of all banks and decided which ones would be allowed to reopen.

The 12th Federal Reserve District, which contained the national California banks, was to return to banking business on Monday, March 13. As the day came closer, the Bank of America officers grew nervous, for they had not received a license to reopen. Frantic telephone calls were made to Washington officials. If the offices of Bank of America failed to open up on Monday, the gigantic bank and its many branches would collapse, spelling certain ruin of its hundreds of thousands of depositors.

It was then discovered that the head of the Federal Reserve Bank in San Francisco, John U. Calkins, who bore a long-time grudge against Giannini and his bank, had given the Treasury Department a year-old report on the Bank of America's financial status, showing its condition just when Giannini regained control. Rushing against a deadline of a few hours, A. P. and his worried officers assembled current figures that demonstrated the bank's return to a state of health. Calkins, unwilling to accept responsibility for keeping the bank closed, was forced to certify that it was solvent. So on that dramatic Monday morning in 1933, the doors of the several hundred branches of Bank of America swung open to the public. Few customers knew how close they had come to disaster. As for A. P., he gave an audible sigh of relief; once again his bank had been saved.

The country slowly returned to a semblance of well-being.

But Giannini increasingly endured frustration in his at-
tempts to expand his business domains as government regulations grew tighter. The Security Exchange Commission
singled out TA for close scrutiny and called hearings. For
years the case dragged on; only in 1947 were the charges
finally dismissed.

Giannini knew well that his time was running out. His
son Virgil died in 1937, his wife in 1941. More and more he
turned over managing reins to younger men, especially to
Mario, who had become president of Bank of America in
1936. Giannini concentrated on preparations for the nation-
wide banking system he had envisaged long before; understandably, he was anxious to see it started before he died.

The Bank of America developed new ways to increase assistance to its customers: like Timeplan, the low-interest loan
program. In 1931, the bank occupied the huge new building
at 300 Montgomery Street in San Francisco. (It served well
for twenty-five years; a still larger modern building was
under construction by the late 1960s.) During World War
II there was a return to prosperity that made happy the heart
of a man who liked to " Be first in everything." In 1945,
Bank of America was indeed first; it had become the largest
privately owned (non-government) bank in the world.

Giannini began to be seen only rarely around his bank—a
sure sign that he was unwell. He died on June 3, 1949, not
long after his seventy-ninth birthday. He left an estate of
$489,278, far more modest than his detractors had ever
suspected. The bulk of the money went to the Bank of
America-Giannini Foundation, which provides scholarships
to bank employees and also promotes medical research.

L. M. Giannini died three years later. Neither Mario nor
his father lived to see the passage of a Congressional bill that

put an end to A. P.'s dreams of nation-wide branch banking. Holding companies were limited to owning only one bank, so the Bank of America separated from Transamerica Corporation. Not long afterwards, TA was disbanded; there no longer was a compelling reason to prolong its life.

But other more important ideas of Amadeo Peter Giannini survived—like his daring, liberal attitude that banks belong to the people who use them, rich and poor alike. This point of view and the services he instituted have become standard offerings in banks everywhere. Giannini also proved conclusively that branch banking was workable in the United States and in many ways preferable.

Most of all, however, there were countless small, purely human accomplishments that A. P. Giannini and his bank had made possible. He firmly believed, and demonstrated, that "A banker should have a hand ready to help everyone worthy of aid when dark days come along."

The Biggest Little Man in the Country

Fiorello H. La Guardia

"I would rather be right than regular."

THE MOST DYNAMIC and colorful mayor ever to occupy a city hall in the United States was an Italian-American whose first name meant "little flower." But a little flower Fiorello H. La Guardia was not; rather, a low-set, chubby, ever-spinning human whirlwind. During a succession of public careers, he devoted all his prodigious energy to the People (always with a capital "P"), who needed a doughty defender.

On December 11, 1882, Fiorello Henry La Guardia was born in New York City, the great metropolis where one day he would be mayor for a dozen years. His father, Achille La Guardia, from southern Italy, had taken his first look at the United States in 1878 while touring as an accompanist for the singer Adelina Patti. He decided to return to this nation that seemed so vital and promising. In Trieste he married a girl of Jewish descent, and the young couple left for New York. There Achille had trouble making a decent, regular living as a musician; his responsibilities increased with the births of a girl, Gemma, and then of Fiorello.

When Fiorello was two years old, his father joined the Army, becoming an infantry band conductor. Achille got a handsome uniform, a small but secure income, and orders to travel. He took his family with him from one post to another. Fiorello's migratory childhood left him with few memories up to the time he was ten years old, when his father was assigned to the Army post at Prescott, a sizable town in central Arizona. Fiorello always considered himself a product of the West. His Arizona years gave him, in his words, a "happy, wholesome boyhood." He liked open spaces, clean air, and a feeling of freedom both physical and spiritual.

In the midst of his pleasant surroundings, however, young Fiorello observed, and loathed, social wrongs: the corruption and exploitation of people, injustice, intolerance, and poverty. "Many of the things on which I have strong feelings," he said later, "were first impressed on my mind during those early days."

As a boy Fiorello saw slick government agents steal money belonging to their defeated, helpless Indian charges. They epitomized the "Politician"—a hack who had won a snug sinecure for services rendered. He watched the "Tinhorns"— the professional gamblers and con men—with their sly schemes cheat gullible people out of life savings by promising them futures of riches. La Guardia would later be relentless in pursuing these "economic vermin," "the scum of society," whether petty gangsters or big-time thugs. He also noticed the large-scale misuse of immigrant labor in mines and industries and in building railroads. Ambitious and unscrupulous entrepreneurs were amassing huge fortunes, giving their thousands of lowly workers little in return for their drudgery and bondage. If Capitalism frequently drew La Guardia's ire, it was because he hated economic exploitation.

Fiorello learned too of a special prejudice against Italians. When an Italian organ-grinder came to town, Achille invited him home for dinner. Now for the first time Fiorello's school-mates noticed that he was an "Eye-talian" too. "A Dago with a monkey!" they teased. "Hey, Fiorello, you're a Dago too. Where's *your* monkey?" (When La Guardia became mayor of New York, he banished hurdy-gurdies and cup-passing musicians from the city's streets, saying that they caused traffic snarls. Privately he did not find them picturesque and enter-taining, but pitiful beggars usually with Italian names who enabled more fortunate citizens to feel superior.)

During the 1890s, Fiorello's father bought issues of the New York *World;* in them Fiorello read of the crusade against Tammany Hall, the powerful political "machine" that the Democratic Party had created to gain and maintain control over New York City's leadership, finances, and law courts. Since New York was his birthplace, Fiorello took great interest in news of the city, although he was growing up far away. Fiorello was appalled by and felt indignant about the revelations in the *World.* "Unlike boys who grew up in the city and who heard from childhood about such things as graft and corruption," he said later, "the amazing disclosures hit me like a shock. I could not understand how the people of the greatest city in the country could put up with the vice and crime that existed there." Tammany Hall began to sym-bolize for him the worst evils in mankind; his early loathing grew rage-sized in those later years when he himself was tus-sling with the Tammany "Tiger."

Even as a child Fiorello was a fighter. Always pint-sized, in those years skinny, he never ran from a fight—except the time he retreated to get a chair from the schoolroom so he could attain his opponent's height. Unconsciously, perhaps, he was in training for a lifetime of battling in the public arena. And he was bound to have fights ahead of him, for he was an idealist, believing in the intrinsic merit of democratic government, in the innate goodness of most people. "I was certain that good people could eliminate bad people from public office," he said.

With his fierce loyalties, Fiorello saw the world in terms of Good and Evil. And whether an offense was slight or enormous, the scandal of a single household or one that was national, even world-wide in scope, La Guardia at full tilt took after the dark forces, thundering abuse and expecting the bystanders to cheer him on. His fighting technique may have been flamboyant, even undignified or rude . . . but nobody ever failed to notice him, and that was what he wanted. A rousing drama displayed to the public those issues for which he passionately lived and fought: truth, liberty, equality, justice; and for everybody, a roof over his head, warm clothes, and three square meals a day.

Fiorello's childhood came to an abrupt end in 1898 with the Spanish-American War. Achille was sent to Florida, where preparations were being made for an invasion of Cuba. Always intensely patriotic, Fiorello tried to join the Army but was rejected. Yet the intrepid fifteen-year-old headed toward the war anyway by persuading a newspaper to hire him as a correspondent. Following his father to Florida, Fiorello there suffered a terrible personal blast to his youthful idealism. Along with thousands of other American soldiers, Achille was poisoned by the "embalmed" beef canned by profit-greedy meatpackers. La Guardia now had another foe: the War Profiteer, who disregarded the welfare of other people while he reaped the rich harvest of government money.

The sick, embittered Achille was given a medical discharge. To start a new life, the La Guardia family returned to Trieste, where they ran a small hotel. In 1901, Achille La Guardia died, and his death marked for Fiorello the most disgusting scandal in American military history.

Now in the Europe of his ancestors, Fiorello La Guardia became a clerk in the American consulate at Budapest. In his spare time, he studied world history and also learned Italian and German, and smatterings of Yiddish and Croatian. If he saw any brilliant future for himself in the American foreign service, it was quickly extinguished by the Consul-General. "He solemnly assured me," Fiorello recalled, "that because I did not have a degree from Harvard I would never get any higher than the menial position of clerk."

But the aggressive, hard-working Italian-American did progress by getting himself appointed the American consular agent in Fiume, Hungary's only seaport. Living at the one-man office—where he was "boss, clerk, and my own messenger"—the twenty-one-year-old Fiorello at once assumed authority and began to shatter precedents and dismiss rigid protocol. The Cunard Lines had started a twice-monthly shipping service from Fiume to the United States, the cargo being principally emigrants. On each trip several thousand people were crowded into steerage; when the steamship returned to Fiume it brought back several hundred hapless passengers rejected for health reasons at Ellis Island.

To spare emigrants the discomforts and expense of a needless long voyage, La Guardia declared that he would not sign the requisite Bill of Health for any ship's departure until all passengers were first examined by a doctor. The steamship company at first balked at the brash young American's ruling, then realized that they had to cooperate with him. As a result, during La Guardia's tenure, Fiume had the lowest immigrant-rejection rate of any European port of embarkation. But in vain did La Guardia suggest to the Immigration Service that other ports adopt similar measures. A plan like his was not instituted until 1919. Through the years, so many of Fiorello's proposals were considered too "radical"; or else they were too simple and obvious for the ponderous motions of bureaucracy.

La Guardia at last realized that to accomplish much in the way of improving the world, he would need a better education. In 1906, he returned to the United States, leaving behind him in Europe his mother and his sister, who had married. He attended night classes at New York University's Law School; and seven days a week, eight hours a day, he worked for the Immigration Service as an interpreter at Ellis Island. The European migration to the United States was then in its floodtide, and Fiorello helped to process that unending stream of immigrants arriving at the rate of 5,000 a day.

Countless domestic dramas were enacted before him. Families so often were told that one or more of their members was unacceptable because of physical or mental defects. A man without the prospect of a job might be rejected as likely to become a public charge; yet, paradoxically, the man next to him could also be excluded if he had obviously arranged for a contract-labor job. La Guardia wrote later of his job: "Our compensation, besides our salaries, for the heartbreaking scenes we witnessed was the realization that a large percentage of these people pouring into Ellis Island would probably make good and enjoy a better life than they had been accustomed to where they came from."

During his last year in the Immigration Service, La Guardia worked as an interpreter at Night Court in Manhattan, where he viewed the widespread graft among policemen and judges. He was disgusted to see the law-enforcers taking advantage, and making fun, of immigrants' naïvete and helplessness. La Guardia refused to be part of any shady transactions. "It was the first, instinctive reaction to dishonesty or indecency that always counted," he said.

La Guardia was graduated from New York University Law School in 1909 and in October was admitted to the New York Bar Association. With only six dollars in his pocket, he resigned from the Immigration Department and set up his own small law office. "But," he wrote later, "I had no particular passion for the practice of the law." His increasing experience in courts of law gave him no pride in his profession. He turned down requests for his services if he did not believe in a prospective client's case; and if he knew of a simpler, cheaper way of obtaining a just settlement, he informed a visitor of it. Soon he earned among lower-class people a reputation for honesty and genuine helpfulness.

La Guardia was asked to represent a labor union in a strike against garment-industry employers, who had long exploited their workers—most of them immigrants laboring in "sweatshop" tenements—and now were refusing to improve working conditions and raise wages. By the hundreds, strikers were hauled off to jail. Fiorello proved his mettle as champion of the poor by entering wholeheartedly into the strikers' cause, even trying to get himself arrested with them for picketing. He uncovered and dispelled all sorts of dirty tactics the manufacturers used in attempting to break the union's strength. When the strikers finally won, La Guardia's name became widely known by both liberals and those with economic grievances.

"I did not accumulate much money," Fiorello said of his early years as a practicing lawyer, "but I managed to live, found time for study and research, and certainly learned a great deal about political and economic conditions in my city." Eager to bring about better conditions, he was drawn, inevitably, into politics. Because of his dislike of New York's Tammany Hall, he became an active member in a local Republican club. He set his sights on a target: the House of Representatives. "Somehow—I did not know how—I had the feeling that someday I would get into Congress," Fiorello said.

Fiorello La Guardia's first chance in politics came up unexpectedly. "Who wants to run for Congress?" the Republican Club's leader asked at a meeting that was deciding the election slate for 1914. "I do!" Fiorello volunteered. "Let's get someone whose name we can spell," said the man recording the candidates' names. But slowly and patiently La Guardia spelled out his full name. In years to come, many people would be unable to spell or pronounce it properly— yet they managed to vote for him.

The Congressional seat in the offing was in the 14th District, a section in lower Manhattan largely populated by Jewish, Italian, and Irish immigrants but also containing the well-to-do neighborhood around Washington Square. The district always went overwhelmingly for Tammany Hall candidates. Any Republican entering the race did so just for the experience, for his defeat was foreordained.

To everybody's surprise, La Guardia took his candidacy seriously and worked hard to win. "We went from corner to corner every night in that district," he recalled, "and we never missed a wedding, a funeral, a christening or any other kind of gathering we could get into." His opponent was the incumbent Congressman Michael Farley, who hardly bothered to campaign. Farley was re-elected—but only by a slim margin of 1,700 votes, a real wonder in the district that usually gave the Democrats a plurality of 15,000. The Republicans noted that La Guardia was a "comer," a man with ability to attract voters, particularly new citizens.

As a reward for a good showing, La Guardia was made a deputy attorney-general by New York State's Republican governor. He leapt at once into the exciting business of obtaining justice for worthy causes. But he soon discovered that no matter what telling facts he mustered, rarely could he bring a case into court, let alone achieve a decision in its favor. "I never realized until this experience," he commented, "how far-reaching special privileges and favors really went."

Rung by rung as he climbed the ladder of politics, Fiorello would see all the shining ideals of his youth tarnished by corrupters and exploiters, men who used power and money to further their own selfish interests. Too many times he saw that men pursued politics for fame, glamor, power, wealth—certainly not out of any love for lofty principles or concern over the fate of little people. He also noticed that judges were generally appointed not for merit but to repay political debts, and they made decisions coincide with the dictates of special factions. In such a system, how could genuine justice be obtained? Thus when La Guardia left the attorney-general's office, he was "wiser and not so innocent." He had also discovered his peculiar niche as a political rebel with an independent way of thinking. "Not to comply and accept the established custom, things as they are," he said, "brands one as an insurgent."

In the midst of an active career, Fiorello found time for close friendships with artists, poets, musicians, union leaders, political workers—liberals all—and with plain working-class people. And he fell in love with Thea Almerigotti, a dress designer from Trieste. But the courtship went slowly, for Fiorello's time was so taken up with politics, and Thea had doubts about marrying a non-Catholic. (La Guardia was raised as an Episcopalian.)

La Guardia naturally assumed that the Republicans would want him to run again in the 14th Congressional District's election in 1916. He learned, however, that the candidacy had been promised to a wealthy young man with good connections. When the irate Fiorello threatened to oppose him in the primary, the Republicans dropped the contender and picked La Guardia. It was the first of many maneuvers on Fiorello's part to get the spot he wanted.

La Guardia proceeded to compaign in the same vibrant style as two years before. This time Tammany Hall took him seriously. But Michael Farley, "the sitting Congressman," paled by comparison with the strident-voiced immigrants' son who, delivering hypnotically drumming speeches in English, Italian, and Yiddish, pledged himself to improving living and working conditions in the district and really giving a forceful and faithful representation in Congress. Knowing that Tammany Hall customarily tampered with election returns, La Guardia had all voting precincts closely guarded. His vigilance paid off; he was elected—with a plurality of 357 votes.

"My dream of a lifetime had come true," La Guardia felt on taking his seat in Congress on March 5, 1917, the first Italian-American to serve there. With typical aplomb he entered the great chamber, looked around him, and chose a seat up front—something freshmen Congressmen simply did not do. The thirty-four-year-old representative from New York was regarded as a "freak" by Washington politicians noting his upset victory in a Democratic stronghold. La Guardia obviously stood for the new immigrant citizens and the urban masses who ultimately might overwhelm the cautious, tradition-bound opinions of the wealthy classes, the farmers, and the small-town dwellers. One need not welcome him or approve of him, but he was there, much seen and much heard. Although nominally a Republican, La Guardia was closer in spirit to the few Progressives in the Capitol, who in that 65th Congress often controlled the outcome of voting split equally between Democrats and Republicans.

Washington, D.C., was very tense at the time of La Guardia's arrival, for the war in Europe, which Americans had tried to avoid, was now pulling them in. President Woodrow Wilson, who had campaigned for peace, could no longer ignore German attacks upon American shipping, and Americans increasingly sympathized with France, England, and Italy. War was imminent, and even before it came, America's lawmakers were busy preparing for it. Although rookie representatives rarely spoke up, Fiorello broke precedent by getting the floor on his second day in Congress and proposing a bill that would impose stiff sentences on manufacturers of defective military provisions—in time of war, the death penalty. "I had to get it off my chest," Fiorello wrote to Thea. "Something has to be done so that lives are not traded for money." It was a debt owed his dead father; but with a swift dismissal, La Guardia's bill was shunted off to a committee, to be ignored and then forgotten.

On April 2, Wilson, addressing a joint session of Congress, asked for a declaration of war against Germany. La Guardia always felt that people and nations should live together in peace; but whenever a just cause propelled his country into war, he was genuinely and fervently patriotic. He voted for war and then for the Selective Service Act—both votes causing him trouble in his heatedly pacifistic district.

La Guardia took a courageous stand during the first session of Congress by objecting to parts of the Espionage Act, which he considered dangerous to the basic American rights of free speech and free assembly. His warnings went unheeded. He also protested a sudden steep rise in food prices while food was still abundant; rents and clothing costs had skyrocketed too, whereas wages had not kept pace. He believed that it was the government's duty within the free-enterprise system to control the prices of such necessaries. "Someday we will come to realize," he said, "that the right to food, shelter, and clothing at reasonable prices is as much an inalienable right as the right to life, liberty, and the pursuit of happiness."

While participating in wartime legislation, La Guardia wanted direct, personal action. "I had told the young men in my district that if I should vote for putting them into the Army, I would go myself," he said. He was among the few Congressmen who did. When the First World War had started in Europe, he had felt that the United States would eventually be drawn in too, so he began to prepare for it by taking flying lessons. Now, in mid-July of 1917, La Guardia enlisted in the Air Division of the Signal Corps and was given a captain's commission. By autumn, he and his company were finishing training at Foggia, Italy—by coincidence, Achille La Guardia's birthplace.

No official blunder, no waste, no ruling detrimental to the welfare of his men seemed to escape Congressman-Captain La Guardia's sharp eyes—and tongue. After the defeat at Caporetto, when Italian morale needed boosting, La Guardia's unit went north to join the Italian Air Force in bombing Austrian industrial and military sites. In between flying sorties, Fiorello gave speeches in principal cities, reassuring Italians of his country's assistance.

In August of 1918, La Guardia was promoted to Major. (He was so proud of the title that in future years many associates used it—or, more simply, "The Maje.")

In October, Fiorello returned to New York to campaign for re-election to Congress. For months, petitions had been circulating in his district to unseat the absentee Congressman. "I am working not only for my district, but for my country," La Guardia had commented. "You might say that if any signers of the petition will take my seat in a Caproni biplane, I shall be glad to resume my upholstered seat in the House." Now, in a fusion effort to combat the considerable strength of the anti-war Socialist Party, the Democrats endorsed the Republican candidate for the 14th District. Resplendent in his uniform, La Guardia easily won the election. Since the war was almost over, he resigned his commission and returned full-time to Congress.

After the Armistice, the temper of the times abruptly changed. Gone now was the warmongering, extremist spirit that had disturbed La Guardia. It was replaced by the feeling, "Let's get the boys home; let's mind our own business from now on." And America's own business, as reflected in Congress during the ensuing decade, was a matter for La Guardia's concern and disgust. With a handful of liberal Senators and Congressmen, La Guardia began a long rearguard action against legislation that he considered defective, discriminatory, or shortsighted.

In 1919, the Republican Party asked La Guardia to run for the office of president of the New York City Board of

Aldermen—the second-highest executive post in the city. He agreed, on the understanding that, if elected, he would be the Republican mayoralty candidate in 1921. When La Guardia won, he began at once to make trouble for all vested interests in the city government. In the flamboyant, outspoken style he was perfecting, he proposed a new law: the hands of any public official found accepting a bribe would be cut off. "And I would also advocate," he amended, "cutting off both hands of the man who gave the bribe." Annoying the city's landlords, he asked for rent controls. He spoke out noisily and angrily against anything or anybody that caused hardship to the People. He offended many prominent, conservative Republicans, who wanted no part of him, especially as prospective mayor. Refused the nomination, Fiorello entered the primary on his own, campaigning for "'Efficient Municipal Management." *The New York Times* sounded the prevalent attitude toward him: "Picturesque, amusing, and impossible."

Fiorello La Guardia had married Thea Almerigotti in 1919. They settled into a Greenwich Village apartment, where they frequently entertained their many close friends, with Fiorello zestfully preparing the *pasta*. Next year their baby girl, Fioretta, was born. But both mother and child were sickly. Fioretta died a year after her birth, and it was discovered that Thea had an advanced case of tuberculosis. Her death came just after Fiorello's defeat in the primary election for the mayoralty.

La Guardia's foes thought that his personal bereavement, combined with political defeat, had brought his public career to an end. But he still showed his fighting spirit when he made his farewell speech as president of the Board of Aldermen: "New York is the richest city in the world, but until every child is fed and every home has air and light and every man and woman a chance for happiness, it is not the city it ought to be." After a long rest in Cuba, Fiorello returned to resume his law practice—and to speak out on all issues that concerned him.

Wanting to get the irrepressible La Guardia back into their camp, yet keep him away from local politics, the Republicans offered him the chance to run for Congress in the 20th Congressional District in east Harlem. La Guardia was eager to get back to Congress; he campaigned energetically in the poverty belt made up largely of Italian and Jewish families. When his Democratic opponent told the Jewish voters that he was anti-Semitic, La Guardia promptly challenged him to a public debate in Yiddish, knowing full well that his Jewish opponent could not speak it.

In this hard-fought campaign La Guardia drew the fervid admiration of a group of young men, many of them Italian, who pledged themselves utterly to him and his victory. Calling themselves the "Gibboni" (the name has various spellings and interpretations, but usually is said to be slang for "swashbucklers"), they were to be at Fiorello's beck and call for years, serving as his body guards, preventing the other side from stuffing ballot-boxes, arranging rallies for their idolized leader, escorting voters to the polls—and frequently playing pranks. Sometimes their appearance and behavior harmed La Guardia's image.

Fiorello won the 1922 Congressional election by a margin of only 254 votes. But he was returned to Congress . . . where he would stay for a decade. La Guardia is generally remembered today as the energetic, impetuous, reform-minded mayor of New York City—as colorful a character as ever appeared in the comic strips he read to his radio listeners during a newspaper strike. Yet his years in the House of Representatives as a "fighting Congressman" may be almost as worthy of public memory. It was La Guardia's characteristic and fate always to be ahead of his times. Or were other politicians behind theirs? The proposals La Guardia propounded vigorously on the House floor were ignored, scorned, or ridiculed by most of his fellow representatives. He wanted minimum wage laws, old-age pensions, workmen's compensation, child-labor laws, the abolition of injunctions in labor disputes; he also advocated public-owned utilities and the freedom of speech for minority political groups. Nowadays, of course, we take most of Fiorello's objectives for granted, because most of them were enacted during the early years of the New Deal, when the Depression forced lawmakers to try new solutions for the nation's economic problems.

In contrast to many other elected representatives in the capital, busy participating in the social life, La Guardia took his job seriously and worked almost a twenty-four-hour day, a seven-day week. When he was not battling some foe or futilely urging some liberal legislation in the House, he was in his office, surrounded by books, papers, and busy assistants, poring over Congressional matters—figuring out ways to block bills he did not like or mapping strategy for the victory of bills he supported.

Fiorello persistently fought against Prohibition. When the Eighteenth Amendment and the Volstead Act went into effect, he maintained that the problems attending alcohol simply could not be legislated out of existence, that prohibition would only beget worse evils from gangsters and corrupt public officials who would prosper from the illicit production, importation, and sale of liquor.

One of La Guardia's biggest fights in Congress came in 1924 over the passage of the National Origins Immigration Bill. For some while many Americans had wanted to limit immigration. America's fabled "melting pot" was boiling over, unable to absorb all at once, without strife and chaos, so many millions of incoming foreigners, each group with its own language, customs, and beliefs. Unemployed Americans resented foreigners with steady jobs. Labor unions hardly welcomed the continuous flow of unskilled immigrants into the country, willing to work for lower wages and put up with deplorable living and working conditions. More and more liberal politicians combined with conservatives and racist reactionaries to shut the "golden door" of America to all but a few. First, immigration from China and Japan was stopped. Then, in 1917, Congress had passed a bill requiring literacy in any immigrant desiring entry.

In 1921, the first quota system was introduced by Congress, but after three years there was clamor for even stricter measures. The total quota was reduced from 358,000 to 165,000, with the quotas for each European country to be determined as 2 per cent of its nationals living in the United States at the time of the 1890 census. The bill quite deliberately weighted the quotas in favor of the "old" immigration from the British Isles, Scandinavia, and Germany, for it was after 1890 that the greatest flow of "new" immigrants came from the "less desirable" countries in eastern and southern Europe.

Eloquently but vainly La Guardia protested against this discrimination against certain national groups. He found nativist prejudice absurd, loathsome, and dangerous. "After all," he asked, "did not every one of us descend from immigrant stock? Some arrived on the Mayflower and many more in the steerage." La Guardia knew well that the immigrants "have in many cases contributed much more to the welfare of this nation than those who look down upon them or turn their noses up at them. Look around you in any part of this country: the immigrants have contributed more than their share to building its power and wealth."

The ease with which the immigration restriction act of 1924 passed through both houses of Congress embittered La Guardia, particularly against the Republican administration under Harding and Coolidge. He broke with the Republican Party by refusing to endorse Coolidge for re-election in 1924, and instead supported the Progressives' candidate, Senator Robert M. LaFollette. "The supreme issue is the encroachment of the powerful few upon the rights of the many," he decided when taking this insurgent stand. "I would rather be right than regular," he said—a good motto for his entire career. Being politically "regular," a good party man, meant subscribing to attitudes and actions he could not approve. Although LaFollette was overwhelmingly defeated, La Guardia—running on the same Progressive ticket—was returned to Congress with a strong plurality. In fact, his district was the only one in the East that supported LaFollette.

While many were talking of the "magic of prosperity," La Guardia saw things differently. People worked hard, but they could not make ends meet. In his own district he organized meat-buyers' strikes to protest high prices. And to provide some drama for Congress as well, one day he got up to give a speech on the subject and from his pocket pulled out a scrawny piece of meat—thirty cents' worth of lamb. This was the sort of performance Fiorello delighted in giving. "It is impossible to enjoy the blessings of liberty on an empty stomach," he said.

La Guardia bitterly attacked Andrew Mellon, the Secretary of the Treasury and one of America's richest men, after he proposed a tax cut on higher incomes—to "encourage business incentive." And when Mellon tried to impose a sales tax on basic commodities, La Guardia's fury knew no bounds: Mellon's tax would hit hardest the people who could least afford it. La Guardia, speaking before the House, said that he would not dispute the financial genius of Mellon or his fellow millionaires. "But can any of them," he asked, "improve on the financial genius of Mrs. Mary Esposito, or Mrs. Rebecca Epstein, or Mrs. Maggie Flynn, who keep house in a city tenement, raise six children on a weekly envelope containing thirty dollars, try to send their children to school warmly and properly clad, pay exorbitant gas and electric bills, and endeavor to provide meat at least once a day for the family? That's financial genius of the highest order."

La Guardia himself had no understanding of people who accumulated money and possessions. He lived simply and frugally and saw the Devil himself in human greed. So "Soak the rich!" became La Guardia's crude battle cry against Mellon's tax. And it worked. Although a majority in both houses of Congress were initially disposed toward the sales tax, under Fiorello's urging they changed their minds and instead placed a tax on luxury items which the poor did not buy.

In other instances too La Guardia rallied Congressmen— as in defeating Henry Ford's purchase of Muscle Shoals in the Tennessee River to produce electricity and fertilizer. La Guardia wanted the government to develop huge hydroelectric projects that would benefit the people themselves, not private industry. Thus he helped reserve for the future one of the New Deal's notable accomplishments: TVA. Another La Guardia triumph was the passage of the Norris-La Guardia Anti-Injunction Bill, which forbade the use of force in settling labor disputes and stopped the "yellow dog" contract in which employers compelled workers to sign pledges not to join unions.

In February of 1929, Fiorello La Guardia married Marie Fischer, who for thirteen years had been his efficient and indispensable secretary, assistant, and campaign director. The marriage was a happy one, and the couple, unable to have their own children, adopted a girl and a boy.

In the same year, Fiorello decided to run for the mayoralty of New York City. Despite the protests of many Republicans, he won the primary. Then he had to oppose the highly popular incumbent mayor, James J. Walker. La Guardia loudly decried the intricate spider's web of graft, vice, and inefficiency in the city government. It was the last heady days of the Roaring Twenties, and New Yorkers, laughing at Fiorello's somber warnings of corruption and economic disaster, merrily followed their Pied Piper—nimblefooted Jimmy Walker. A week before the election came the great stock market crash, but it hardly affected the voting. La Guardia, the chubby, gloomy little oracle, lost by half a million votes.

"Tammany Hall will take it as an approval, that the people do not want a reform mayor," La Guardia said of his stunning defeat. But he felt that people had simply refused to believe him. "I know I made some startling charges about crime and politics and about money from the underworld," he commented; "but mark my words, in the next few years we'll prove these charges!"

In 1930, Governor Franklin D. Roosevelt asked Judge Samuel Seabury to investigate the New York City Magistrates' Courts. Seabury's zealous inquiry began to uncover unsavory trails between criminals and city officials. Since his investigation involved a series of courtroom dramas, New Yorkers could no longer remain ignorant of the corruption in their midst. Governor Roosevelt finally asked Mayor Walker himself to go on the stand and answer Seabury's questions. Backed into a corner during the hearings, Walker resigned as mayor of New York City in September of 1932.

Meanwhile, the country was sinking deeper into the Depression. As the situation grew desperate, Congressional liberals like La Guardia urged measure after measure as remedies: government-sponsored public works that would create many jobs; government-insured bank savings accounts; unemployment insurance; a shorter work week. But President Hoover usually resisted their efforts to make the federal government take an active role. Fiorello believed that the nation needed a strong leader to introduce radical new legislation, so he wholeheartedly backed Franklin D. Roosevelt's candidacy. The Democratic landslide that propelled FDR into the presidency operated against the insurgent Republican La Guardia who had supported him; Fiorello lost in his own re-election to Congress by a thousand votes. He tried to take his defeat philosophically and spoke now of doing other things—unthinkable things, like retiring.

But La Guardia was not through yet, for he still had to attend the "lame duck" session of Congress. Realizing that important legislation must be started even before he assumed office, Roosevelt wanted a forceful, liberal leader in the

House to propose and push through new bills. He chose La Guardia as his "advance man," which guaranteed that Fiorello's last weeks in Congress were busy and noisy and full of conflict—just as he liked them. At long last, if only briefly, he was doing something to help America's "little people."

In the spring of 1933, Fiorello H. La Guardia, fifty years old, was out of public office and back in private law practice in New York. He began to assess his chances for the coming mayoralty nominations. Since Judge Seabury had lifted the blinders from New Yorkers' eyes, the political climate had changed. Mayor John O'Brien, Walker's successor, became the laughingstock of the town and proved how closely Tammany controlled City Hall when he replied to a reporter asking him who his new police commissioner would be, "I don't know, I haven't heard yet."

Influential New Yorkers wanting good government—the "Googoos"—formed a Fusion party that would appeal to reform-minded Democrats, liberal Republicans, and various independent groups. Although La Guardia was willing and eager to tackle the job of cleaning up and administering the world's biggest and most complex city, it became obvious that the Fusion leaders did not want him. They all wanted the hero of New York, Judge Seabury, to run for mayor. Seabury, however, declined—and insisted that they choose La Guardia instead. "This is the man who would give New York honesty in its government," he declared.

The fight for the mayor's seat was furious and fascinating. Behind the scenes, President Roosevelt split the Democratic vote down the middle by encouraging the formation of a reform-Democratic slate to fight against Tammany Hall's candidate, incumbent Mayor O'Brien. Fiorello won by a margin of 250,000 votes over the reform-Democratic contender; it is doubtful whether he would have won had the Democratic vote not been divided.

"Now we have a *mayor*," said Judge Seabury when he heard of Fiorello's victory. La Guardia was the first citizen of Italian ancestry to win such a high elective office. He took the oath of office in Seabury's library after midnight on January 1, 1934. Then he shook the Judge's hand, kissed his wife, posed for photographers, and told reporters: "Our theory of municipal government is an experiment to show that a non-partisan, non-political, honest, clean government is possible."

After a few hour's sleep, La Guardia went to work. "Clean house and clean it thoroughly," he said, giving his administration's key command, and New York began experiencing all in a rush the lightning-and-thunder storm that was Fiorello.

Swiftly, with all the power of his office, La Guardia struck out at everything and everybody he detested: the "lousy crooks" and "cheap tinhorns," the corrupt office-holders and lazy bureaucrats who had long made a mockery of government by and for all the people. Fiorello seemed everywhere at once. He might suddenly swoop down upon a Lower Eastside city relief office and stand in line as a short, anonymous person, to observe the slow-moving, condescending civil servants at work. When he had seen enough, he stepped out and began issuing orders and firing the worst offenders, who unknowingly had been parading their ineptitude in front of their new mayor. . . . Or, going unannounced into a small precinct police station, La Guardia might begin giving brisk commands. "Just who do you think you are?" a policeman would ask. "Personally, I am nobody much," Fiorello would reply almost humbly and then switch to a loud, firm tone. "But the job I happen to hold is the Mayor of the City of New York—"

Fiorello poked into innumerable matters large and small. He inspected garbage trucks and dumps; he gave speeches, cut ribbons, and wielded shovels at ground-breaking ceremonies; he read and acted upon the many letters that poured in daily from citizens with suggestions or complaints; he turned every city department upside down and gave it a good shaking. Every day a dozen little blasts or one great one rocked City Hall as La Guardia scolded his commissioners or yelled at his assistants, letting off steam over matters he felt had been poorly handled.

As a Congressman, Fiorello had only a small office staff to cajole, berate, and perform for; now he had thousands of employees to oversee and a city with seven million inhabitants to enthrall. In some ways the explosive La Guardia may have been temperamentally unsuited for his job as chief administrator of a huge city; but he was, nevertheless, a skilled politician with a sure sense of what his people liked and wanted in him. He reduced issues to the simple vernacular of working-class people, distressing those who expected a mayor always to present a silk-hatted dignity in public; he spoke bluntly and plainly so that everybody could understand what he was for and what he was against. And when he charged around town in his broad-brimmed black stetson hat—his trademark—he got things done. People spoke of him intimately as "Butch," "The Little Flower," or "The Hat"; his enemies found less affectionate nicknames. One could depend on him to react against any hint of vice or injustice or to news of one family's being hungry or homeless or cold. Outspoken, vividly human, ever-active, Mayor La Guardia made good copy for the newspapers. Since he was always at the center of any conflict, nobody was indifferent to him; everything he did was observed and talked about.

Fiorello had always shown a flair for the dramatic. Now, as mayor, with the whole city of New York as his stage, he exulted in a multitude of roles. He rode fire engines to fires, hurrying into burning buildings to make his own inspections. He confiscated gamblers' slot machines, smashed them with a sledge hammer, then hurled the pieces into the river. Playfully, he conducted the city's orchestras.

During the Depression, New York received large funds through government agencies such as the Public Works Administration. La Guardia applied them to job-creating, municipal-improvement projects like parks, bridges, schools, public markets, post offices, highways, and the airport which today bears his name. He also supported many Federal Arts Projects in his city.

"My first qualification for this great office," La Guardia said when he became Mayor, "is my monumental personal ingratitude." He declared that, "You can't be a good mayor and a good fellow." He tried to make his appointments on the basis of merit, not as rewards for political support, as the patronage system traditionally dictated. Inevitably, Fiorello made foes as well as friends. He had offended Republican office-seekers. Politically powerful people found his ideas dangerously radical, his actions boorish. In the mayoralty election of 1937, Judge Seabury again had to force the Republican-Fusion movement to re-endorse La Guardia. "Nobody wants me but the people," said Fiorello as the politicians forecast his defeat. And he was right: the people re-elected him, this second victory making him the first "reform" mayor of New York City ever to be returned to office.

Since his post was now considered second in importance only to the President of the United States, La Guardia began to look like an attractive candidate for the coming 1940 presidential election, for either major party. "America's Number One Mayor" took numerous trips to other cities, where he always drew enthusiastic crowds. A San Franciscan cheered him as "the biggest little man in the country."

Meanwhile in Europe another world war was building up. La Guardia was known to be critical of Mussolini, for a time regarded by many admiring Italian-Americans—who did not have to obey his edicts—as another Garibaldi leading Italy to new glories. But Fiorello could not speak frankly in public about Il Duce; it would have meant political suicide, since a big portion of his support came from the Italian population in the city—and he wanted to stay in office. He was not so cautious in his attitude toward the German totalitarian state. He openly referred to Hitler as "the brown shirt fanatic who is menacing the peace of the world," and boldly denounced the Nazis.

Indirectly, Hitler and Mussolini put an end to La Guardia's national political aspirations. With the nation poised on the brink of war, FDR decided to run for an unprecedented third term. A loyal supporter and a lively campaigner, Fiorello probably hoped to be tapped for the vice-presidential spot. When the possibility was mentioned to Roosevelt, he remarked, "There is still a great deal of prejudice against one who has a foreign name." For a while it seemed likely that La Guardia would be appointed Secretary of War to serve in a war-preparing, bipartisan cabinet, but certain political leaders expressed displeasure, so Fiorello again was bypassed. La Guardia—with his great energy, his incorruptibility, an interest in details, a liking for personal inspections, and his hatred for war profiteering—would doubtless have done an admirable job.

So La Guardia stayed on in New York and campaigned for a third term in 1941. Like the Cheshire cat, the Tammany tiger sometimes seemed to disappear except for its grin. La Guardia now wanted to remind the voters that the tiger, symbolizing municipal corruption, was still there, ready to pounce if Fiorello did not win. So to give added drama to his speech-making around town, La Guardia transported a caged tiger with him. And when the tiger roared, he exclaimed: "He's hungry, he's had no graft in years!" In this election Roosevelt directly supported him. "Mayor La Guardia and his administration," he said, "have given to the city the most honest and, I believe, the most efficient municipal government of any within my recollection." Again, La Guardia captured the mayoralty.

Roosevelt had put La Guardia in charge of the new Office of Civil Defense. But what with traveling frequently down to Washington, running City Hall, and campaigning for re-election, Fiorello was unwisely scattering his attention. Several months after America's entry in World War II, La Guardia resigned from his Civil Defense post to return to being the full-time mayor of America's largest port city, which sent out much of the provisions and armaments for the Allies in Europe and North Africa. His big problems now were the housing, food, and fuel shortages; a soaring high cost of living; improving the city's civil defense; fund-raising campaigns; and doing something about war-caused labor shortages in city jobs and vital industries.

During the early days of the war Fiorello began his popular "Talks to the People" radio program. Every Sunday at noon, greeting his citizens with "Patience and fortitude!" the squeaky-voiced mayor would begin to chat. He told New Yorkers how the war was going, gave them recipes for economical Italian meals, sounded out as usual against "tinhorns" and crooks, reminisced, and lectured on the evils of gambling. Fiorello rarely failed to be edifying—and entertaining.

But his patriotic blood had been stirred, and La Guardia wanted to get into real action. After making his feelings known in Washington, he was led to believe that a commission as brigadier general was forthcoming and he might be asked to administer Allied-occupied Italy. Yet his expectation was disappointed as Washington bowed to important military people who did not want Fiorello among them, as well as to influential New Yorkers who liked La Guardia and wanted to keep him.

World War II came to a close just as the New York mayoralty race was coming up again. The Republican party refused to endorse La Guardia because of his chronic insurgency. Although La Guardia still had many loyal supporters and Judge Seabury was proposing another Fusion ticket, Fiorello declined to run again. He did not wish to court defeat; he was tired and no longer was stimulated by the challenge of his job. "Twelve years as Mayor is enough for anybody," he said. Telling his radio listeners of his decision, he added: "As I look back, I see a sense of great comfort. . . . You gave me a job and I did it." His example had encouraged reform-minded public citizens in cities throughout the nation; he was not likely to be forgotten for a long while.

The Democratic candidate, William O'Dwyer, won the election. On New Year's Day of 1946, La Guardia waved his wide black hat at City Hall and drove away in his Ford as a private citizen. Hardly ready to retire, La Guardia kept six secretaries busy at his office in the RCA building. He wrote editorials and a regular column for newspapers, appeared on another radio show in which he commented on the doings—usually political—around his city, and wondered what new tasks lay ahead. Early in 1946, he was appointed Director-General of the United Nations Rehabilitation and Relief Agency, in charge of feeding and resurrecting the war-ravaged countries of Europe, North Africa, and Asia. Now the general of "a great army of mercy," La Guardia was truly in his element. When the work of UNRRA was turned over to the United Nations at the end of the year, Fiorello returned to New York from his wide travels, finding everywhere around him—in concrete and steel or on the faces of the people who recognized him—the evidence of his years as mayor.

He may have been thinking of starting a new career, where he could recharge his physical and spiritual batteries. Perhaps he should now try the Senate. . . . In May of 1947, Fiorello La Guardia was given the One World Award, which included a paid trip around the world. At the ceremony at Carnegie Hall, La Guardia confessed that he was too busy to take the journey—and too ill. The perennial pugilist was losing his battle against cancer. Yet he kept as busy as ever; even when bed-ridden he dictated his memoirs, advised his friends in political life, and composed the expected letters of protest over a variety of public matters.

On September 20, 1947, the 5-5-5-5 bell clanged at the New York City Fire Department—a signal that meant the death of a fireman on duty or of an important city official. This time it rang for the tough little mayor who used to ride zestfully on fire trucks.

Columbus to the Atomic Age

Enrico Fermi

"The Italian navigator has just landed in the New World."

I N AUGUST of 1945, the two atomic bombs dropped on Japan brought World War II to a swift and dramatic end, explosively revealed a fantastic new source of power, and ushered into world-wide fame an Italian-born physicist who had contributed much to the development of atomic energy. If the atom bomb had a "father," it surely was Enrico Fermi.

Released violently as a weapon, atomic energy had the fearful force that leveled Hiroshima and Nagasaki and killed hundreds of thousands of people. But the same vast energy, harnessed for peaceful purposes, could start to serve mankind in an amazing variety of ways.

By leading the world into the Atomic Age, Enrico Fermi changed it as significantly as Columbus did 450 years before him. Both men were navigators into new worlds whose voyages radically altered the course of civilization. Columbus was a mariner who dealt with things readily perceptible to man: land and ocean, wind and stars. Fermi was a nuclear physicist who through theory and experimentation diligently charted the intricate structure and complex behavior of minute atoms, the basic building blocks of matter, of which man is made and by which he is surrounded. Fermi epitomized the twentieth-century explorer: a creative scientist working on projects which seem abstruse and highly specialized to laymen, but making discoveries that often change our lives.

Enrico Fermi was born in Rome on September 29, 1901. For centuries his ancestors had farmed the land close to Piacenza in the Po Valley. Fermi's grandfather, however, had been secretary to the Duke of Parma; his father joined the rapidly developing railroad business, becoming a division supervisor in Rome. After a late marriage, Alberto Fermi's children came in quick succession: Maria, Giulio, then Enrico. The two boys were inseparable; both had a precocious, inquiring, and inventive intelligence. When Giulio suddenly died in 1915, Enrico was heartbroken and found solace only in intense study, as though he would now have to fulfill his brother's destiny too.

Enrico was drawn particularly to physics. A family friend lent him books, encouraged his interests, gave him special problems to work out, and advised him to study at the Reale Scuole Normale Superiore at Pisa—a college for outstanding students. Partly because of his lucid and erudite examination paper on the subject of vibrating strings, Fermi obtained a scholarship. Baffled by such knowledge in a mere student—a young one at that—one of the judges summoned Enrico. After their meeting he called young Fermi "exceptional."

Scholastically remarkable, Enrico still was a normal university student who delighted in sports, parties, mountain climbing, and mischief-making. And since the competitive spirit was strong in him, he tried to win every game, sing the most melodiously, be the first to reach a mountaintop, and contrive the wickedest pranks. Fermi found a keen competitor and good friend in Franco Rasetti, another brilliant physics student. Pisa was an inspirational location for aspiring physicists, for there Galileo had conducted his famous experiments in determining the laws of falling bodies and of the pendulum.

The physics professor gave Fermi and Rasetti freedom to pursue their own experiments. He also asked Enrico to teach him the new theoretical physics introduced by Albert Einstein in his theory of relativity and in his quantum theory regarding the absorption or radiation of energy by matter. Already Fermi was becoming known as a superb teacher.

In July of 1922, Enrico Fermi became a Doctor in Physics, graduating *magna cum laude*. His special field was to be in the new nuclear physics; he had written his thesis on his experimental work with X-rays—the electromagnetic radiation discovered by William Roentgen toward the end of the nineteenth century.

Fermi received a fellowship to study at Göttingen with the German physicist Max Born, who gathered around him a group of talented young scientists, many to become world-famous. Afterwards, Fermi taught mathematics at the University of Rome, a year later joining Rasetti at the University of Florence, where he was an instructor in mathematics and physics and also did theoretical work. A statistical paper, "On the Quantization of a Perfect Monatomic Gas," established Fermi's reputation in the physics profession.

Meanwhile in Rome, Italian politics and science were being transformed. In 1922, Benito Mussolini's Fascist troops had entered the city and seized control of the government, reducing King Victor Emmanuel III to a puppet ruler. Professor Orso Mario Corbino, head of the physics department at the University of Rome, was an influential senator, though not a Fascist. Envisaging a school of physics in Rome that would gain the respect and admiration of the whole scientific world, Corbino wanted to have Enrico Fermi at the nucleus. In 1926, Corbino was permitted to create a new chair in theoretical physics at the University of Rome. In the competitive examination Fermi naturally placed first. Franco Rasetti also got a position, and the two young men who had worked together since student days made up the primary members of the "School of Rome" physics team that would fulfill Corbino's dreams.

Enrico had devised a formula for the perfect wife for him: tall, blonde, strong, athletic, intelligent, of peasant stock, and non-religious. When he married Laura Capon in 1928, his neat eugenics theories flew out the window, for she was short, dark, not especially athletic or robust, city-bred, and of Jewish parentage. And although she was quite intelligent, her mind tended to balk at Enrico's pronouncements. "It is evident that in a nonuniformly accelerated motion, the ratio of the speed to the time is not constant," he might state. "It is *not* evident," his bride would object.

But if Laura could not fully comprehend or just accept "on faith" certain complexities or axioms in theoretical physics, at least Fermi's growing group of physicists did. As prime leader he was dubbed "The Pope," and the others were assigned appropriate positions in a philosophical hierarchy.

In 1929, Fermi was chosen as one of the first members of the new Royal Academy of Italy, and with the high honor went the title of "Excellency" and a gorgeous uniform. Fermi seemed embarrassed by both, declining to use "Excellency" before his name and covering his uniform by a cloak when he went to official gatherings.

In the summer of 1930, the Fermis took their first trip to the United States, where Enrico lectured at the University of Michigan. Fermi made four more visits in the following years, while his wife remained at home, busy caring for their two children, Nella and Giulio. Fermi's liking for the United States grew as he became disillusioned with conditions in Italy. Many people had initially welcomed Mussolini's dictatorship as a means of settling the postwar chaos and preparing the country for a truly democratic regime. But the Fascist government got farther and farther away from democracy. On returning to Italy from America, Fermi would talk about emigrating; but his wife, reluctant to leave her homeland, still hoped that the situation in Italy would improve. Then, as Enrico resumed his work at the University, he almost drew a curtain across the disturbing world outside his laboratory. He was busy there.

In 1932, Fermi had learned of the British physicist James Chadwick's identification of the neutron—the particle within the atomic nucleus which, unlike the proton, carries no electric charge. Two years later, Frederic and Irene Joliot-Curie in France were the first to produce artificial radioactivity, by bombarding elements with alpha particles—the large, positive-charged nuclear particles emitted in radiation. Fermi decided to bombard elements with neutrons, which he believed would be more effective nuclear projectiles than alpha particles, for they traveled faster and farther and were less easily halted. By hitting the nucleus of an atom, a neutron could dislodge protons and thus create artificial radioactivity.

Assisted by his physics team, Fermi gathered together samples of the ninety-two known elements, from hydrogen to uranium. Fermi's main problem was getting enough neutrons to work with. Radioactive substances release alpha particles spontaneously in large quantities; but neutrons could be obtained only indirectly, through bombarding a substance like beryllium with alpha particles. And it would take about 100,000 alpha particles to yield a single neutron. A gram of precious radium at the city health department, emitting radioactive radon gas as it disintegrated, was Fermi's source for alpha particles. He constructed a "neutron gun," a primitive but serviceable device, by mixing radon with beryllium in a small gas tube.

Fermi also built his own Geiger counter so he could detect and measure any radioactivity obtained in the neutron-bombarded elements. Kept away from the other equipment, it was placed in a room down a long hallway. Since any radioactivity produced might last for only a minute or two, the physicists snatched up the elements and rushed them down the corridor to the Geiger counter, inevitably becoming involved with Fermi in a foot race. One day an elegantly dressed Spanish scientist came to the physics building to meet "Sua Excellenza Fermi." There the visitor saw two madmen in dirty lab coats noisily speeding along, carrying strange objects. When one of the rowdy, untidy sprinters turned out to be His Excellency Fermi, the Spaniard could scarcely hide his disillusionment. But, as Fermi's wife remarked of him, "Enrico has always given attention to performance and disregarded appearance."

Fermi's neutron experiments at first yielded nothing. As he painstakingly worked with the first eight elements on the periodic table, he produced not a trace of radioactivity. But he persisted. When he exposed fluorine to his neutron gun, the Geiger counter clicked, indicating that the substance had become radioactive. With increasing excitement now, the physicists pursued their work, creating artificial radioactivity in a number of heavier elements. They also found that elements formed new radioactive forms or isotopes, or even changed into neighboring elements on the periodic table.

Fermi discovered another interesting—and ultimately important—phenomenon. If a "moderator" rich in hydrogen, like water or paraffin, was placed between the neutron source and the bombarded element, the radioactivity produced would be much greater than normal. A dramatic demonstration was made in a goldfish pond behind the physics building, in which the neutron source and a chunk of silver were placed far from each other; when retrieved, the silver set the Geiger counter to rapid clicking—indicating a radioactivity a hundred times greater than that obtained outside the water. Fermi theorized that the neutron projectiles, as they knocked against the protons in the hydrogen atoms, were slowed— just as the speed of a billiard ball is decreased after it hits other balls. These slow neutrons were more easily captured by nuclei, causing increased displacement of protons in the bombarded element, thus making the substance unusually radioactive.

Fermi came finally to the last known element: uranium. A variety of radioactive substances was produced when uranium was bombarded by neutrons; one in particular defied identification. Working with makeshift laboratory equipment on tiny quantities of chemicals—and being physicists rather than chemists specializing in chemical identification— Fermi and his assistants were baffled. Fermi thought it possible that he had produced element number 93.

Senator Corbino spoke in public of the probability that Fermi had created and discovered a new element. Although

Corbino himself was cautious, the Fascist press was eager to claim the splendors of Italian scientists working under Il Duce's rule; Fermi's experiment made world headlines. Fermi tried to maintain a purely objective attitude and stated: "The principal purpose of this research is not to produce a new element—but to study the general phenomenon."

Scientists learning of Fermi's work also tended to reserve judgment on this supposed new, man-made element. But in France, England, America, and Germany, chemists and physicists, with whatever equipment they had or could devise, repeated and varied Fermi's experiments with uranium. At the University of California in Berkeley, where Ernest Lawrence had built the first cyclotron, a gigantic magnet that accelerated charged atomic particles, scientists had a much more powerful source for neutrons than Fermi's neutron "gun." With it they began to search for other man-made elements. While other scientists continued to pursue the mystery of uranium bombardment, Fermi's own research with it came to a standstill. His physics team broke up; some men left for other Italian universities, others went into exile abroad. Fermi again concentrated on theoretical and statistical work away from laboratory experimentation.

In September of 1938, Enrico Fermi learned that he had received the Nobel Prize for Physics. The citation read: "To Enrico Fermi of Rome for his identification of new radioactive elements produced by neutron bombardment and his discovery, made in connection with this work, of nuclear reactions effected by slow neutrons." On the same day, the Fermis heard of new racial laws that discriminated against the Jews in Italy. Laura Fermi's passport was taken away, but an influential friend managed to get it returned to her without having JEW stamped upon it—which would have prevented her from leaving the country.

The Fermis had already decided to live in America, but only their closest friends knew of it. The official reason given for Enrico Fermi's departure from Italy in late 1938 was his acceptance of the Nobel Prize at Stockholm, then a half-year's visit to Columbia University in New York. Since Italians were permitted to carry only fifty dollars abroad, the $50,000 prize was especially welcome to the Fermis. They took their last fond looks at Rome and boarded a train that sped them northward. At the German border they felt a few moments of panic as a Nazi guard scrutinized their papers. The proper visa was found at last, and the Fermis were waved through, on their way to Stockholm—and freedom. At the Nobel Prize ceremony Fermi demonstrated his independence of Mussolini's edicts: he neglected to give a Fascist salute to the King of Sweden and shook hands with him instead. When the incident was reported in the Italian newspapers, it became clear that Fermi had gone for good.

In December of 1938, the ship taking the Fermis to America arrived in New York harbor. While the passengers gazed at the Statue of Liberty, Enrico said with a smile, "We have founded the American branch of the Fermi family." He had hardly touched shore when the famous Danish physicist Niels Bohr arrived on a visit. He had portentous news: German scientists had proved that the uranium atom could be split apart during neutron bombardment. For years physicists had maintained that the atomic nucleus essentially was indivisible; now they would have to revise their thinking. Fermi's elusive, possible "element 93" turned out to be barium; with about half the atomic weight of uranium, it was one of various lighter elements found in minute quantities after uranium atoms split. Niels Bohr told how two German researchers, Hahn and Strassman, had sent word of their discovery to their friend and former colleague, Lise Meitner, a Jewish physicist who had fled from Germany. Meitner theorized that a prodigious quantity of energy would be released during the splitting phenomenon, which she named "fission." Realizing that such a potential source of power would be highly dangerous in Hitler's hands, she hurried to tell Bohr, just as he was leaving for America, of the Germans' uranium work.

Enrico Fermi had been the first to split the uranium atom in his Rome laboratory in 1934, but he failed to recognize it at the time. It is one of the luckiest oversights in world history. Had he realized then what had happened, and published his discovery, German scientists would have had a head start of almost five years in which to develop atomic energy and produce weapons that could virtually rule the world. Although scientists of other nations would surely have studied nuclear fission, probably only the German government in those years would have paid for the great cost of atomic research. When a science reporter asked Fermi about this oversight, no wonder he said, "I am glad I missed."

Bohr's news excited Fermi. Putting aside other projects, he began to study neutrons again; he seemed to think and talk of little else than uranium fission. Fermi now laid the foundation for the future development of atomic energy by advancing a novel idea. In halting, heavily accented English he explained it to a gathering of scientists at Columbia: "The neutron enters and causes an instability in the uranium nucleus and it splits apart. A great deal of energy is released. . . . But the circumstances are those in which, in all probability, neutrons will be emitted as well, and this is at the root of the matter. For if the neutrons are emitted in greater number than they are absorbed, a chain reaction will be possible and the way to a new source of energy will have been found."

Fermi was thus proposing the possibility of the "chain reaction": when one uranium atom split by a neutron divides in two and emits two neutrons, which in turn split two uranium atoms, which then emit four neutrons—a mounting, self-sustaining process that would halt only when all the uranium atoms have been split by, or have captured, the stray neutrons.

Yet the nature of uranium posed a big problem. The element has two principal isotopes, one containing a mass of 238, the other of 235. U 238 makes up more than 99 per cent of natural uranium; but only U 235 is fissionable. There was no easy method of separating them, to obtain quantities of U 235 large enough to test whether a chain reaction was possible.

Fermi believed, however, that a chain reaction might occur in a large, specially constructed pile made up of chunks of natural uranium interspersed with a moderating material that would slow down the speed of neutrons released in the fission of the first U 235 atoms at the pile's center. Slow neutrons, less easily captured by the nuclei of U 238 atoms, could split other U 235 atoms, to emit still more neutrons. Within this pile it should also be possible to control a chain reaction and avoid a violent explosion.

At Columbia University Fermi and his associates began to plan for the construction of this "atomic pile." As a moderator, Fermi chose graphite—almost pure carbon—as the best and most practical material, and in a room in the physics building the physicists began to build graphite bricks in various arrangements around a neutron source, to study on a small scale different shapes for their atomic pile.

During 1939, scientists in the United States and England feared that the Germans were already well ahead of them in atomic research. It was time for the free nations to do something. First of all, they must impose some sort of censorship on their work—contrary to the very nature of science, which normally is open and international in its associations. Leo Szilard, a Hungarian physicist who was Fermi's colleague at Columbia, persuaded other researchers not to discuss publicly or publish in journals any information about their work with nuclear fission.

The Columbia scientists decided to tell the United States government of their project and hopefully obtain support for it; the expense of procuring enough uranium and pure graphite to achieve a chain reaction would be far beyond their means. Only the government had such funds—and it would benefit most from their success were they actually able, as Fermi predicted, to develop an explosive that would make a mere pound of U 235 a million times more powerful than the same weight of TNT.

After a few discouraging initial encounters with officials, Szilard decided to go to the very top. He got his friend Albert Einstein—a refugee from Nazi Germany now settled at Princeton—to write the now-famous letter to President Roosevelt; it was signed on August 2, 1939, and delivered some weeks later by a distinguished emissary. "Some recent work by E. Fermi and L. Szilard . . . leads me to expect that the element uranium may be turned into a new and important source of energy in the immediate future," the letter began. Telling the President about the possibility of achieving a nuclear chain reaction, he went on: "This new phe-

nomenon would also lead to the construction of bombs."
Making it clear that such bombs could cause vast destruction,
he then warned that the Germans were diligently pursuing
their own uranium research.

Roosevelt appointed a Uranium Committee to study the
situation, and the War Department gave $6,000 to Fermi for
the purchase of uranium and graphite. When the first ship-
ment of graphite arrived at Columbia, Fermi and his co-
workers toted around fifty-pound chunks of the slippery
black substance that rubbed off on their clothes, hands, and
faces and made them look like coal miners. They finally hired
the football team to do the manual labor. "After all, we were
thinkers," Fermi commented.

The scientists were still making little headway. They
needed much more than a committee and a few thousand
dollars. They were hearing of ominous happenings in
Europe. A whole group of German physicists were concen-
trating upon atomic research; the Nazis had taken over the
rich uranium mines in Czechoslovakia and had captured the
world's only heavy-water plant, in Norway. Time was running out. France fell, England was under heavy attack, and
the United States, soon and inevitably, would be drawn into
the world war. On December 6, 1941—the day before Pearl
Harbor—Roosevelt and his science advisers decided to support atomic research to the hilt, making all needed funds
available to the nuclear physicists. Arthur H. Compton, a
Nobel Prize physicist at the University of Chicago, was appointed director of the Uranium Project, and was very interested in Fermi's work. Scientists needed proof that a
nuclear chain reaction could be achieved. If so, an atomic
bomb might ultimately be feasible. And if Fermi's atomic
pile really worked, Compton believed it could produce, as

a by-product, the newly-discovered, man-made element, plutonium. Formed in minute quantities from the fission of U 235, plutonium was fissionable too—and potentially as explosive.

In July of 1942, the Fermis—officially listed as "enemy aliens"—moved to Chicago, where the materials for Fermi's atomic pile had already been transferred. He joined other renowned scientists in the secret work at the "Metallurgical Laboratory," the center for atomic research established at the University of Chicago. The squash court beneath the west stands of Stagg Field, the abandoned football stadium, was the only large room available for building a pile that might be over twenty feet high. There, starting in the fall of 1942, scientists in smudged work clothes scurried back and forth, carrying heavy but precious burdens, wearing goggles to protect their eyes from the greasy black dust that filled the air as power saws cut the graphite bricks to size. Their work was infernal-looking to the few outsiders permitted to enter and work or observe. For six weeks Fermi calmly, good-humoredly, and patiently gave directions for erecting a bulky sphere of graphite bricks around chunks of natural uranium—the structure supported by a wooden framework.

In early December, the Fermis gave a party for "Met Lab" scientists. As the guests arrived, each man congratulated Enrico, thoroughly mystifying his wife. What had he done? Laura asked. "Nothing special—he is a smart guy," she was told. The one lady physicist at the Met Lab, sympathetic yet mischievous, whispered, "He has sunk a Japanese admiral." Although dubious, Laura could only conclude that at the Met Lab her husband had devised a secret, deadly ray.

But what had Enrico Fermi really done that day? Laura would have to wait several years before finding out. Today at the University of Chicago a bronze plaque near the spot commemorates Fermi's deed: ON DECEMBER 2, 1942 MAN ACHIEVED HERE THE FIRST SELF-SUSTAIN-ING CHAIN REACTION AND THEREBY INITIATED THE CONTROLLED RELEASE OF NUCLEAR EN-ERGY.

Fermi's atomic pile had reached the "critical size"—or contained enough fissionable uranium to be capable of chain-reacting—somewhat earlier than expected, so the sphere remained flat at its top. On the morning of December 2 the scientists assembled to see whether this first, rudimentary nuclear reactor would work as Fermi said it would. Spectators stood on a balcony to the side of the pile; there Fermi, like an admiral on a ship's bridge, was ready to command his experiment. Below them on the floor was the young physicist George Weil, with his hand on a cadmium rod that would control the release of fission. Perched on top of the pile itself was the "suicide squad"—three young men with buckets of cadmium solution to douse on the nuclear "fire" in case it got out of control.

Following Fermi's instructions, inch by inch Weil withdrew the rod from the center of the pile. With mounting excitement the scientists on the balcony checked instruments recording the increasing neutron activity within the pile. Many—despite their faith in Fermi—were nervous. The pile was working, yes . . . but perhaps it would suddenly explode; or maybe some insidious, unsuspected radiation would kill them all. Fermi, however, remained confident and calm, busily calculating with his small, ever-handy slide rule the intensity of each new release of energy.

No matter how absorbing an experiment might be, Fermi rarely forsook a regular schedule. So in the midst of the tense excitement, he said, "Let's go to lunch." Afterwards the group reassembled and continued the experiment. Fermi finally figured that the next withdrawal of the rod would elicit the hoped-for chain reaction. "Pull it out another foot," he told Weil. Soon—at 3:30 P.M.—the needle following the neutron activity moved on a steep, steadily upward course. Fermi had produced the world's first nuclear chain reaction; and now he kept it under strict control. "When Enrico stood before that silent monster, he was its acknowledged master," said his friend and associate Herbert Anderson of that dramatic day. "Whatever he commanded, it obeyed. When he called for it to come alive and pour forth its neutrons, it responded with remarkable alacrity; and when at his command it quieted down again, it had become clear to all who watched that Fermi had indeed unlocked the door to the Atomic Age."

The news of Fermi's feat traveled quickly but discreetly. Dr. Compton telephoned James Conant, one of the government's foremost science advisers, and cryptically relayed the good news: "You'll be interested to know that the Italian navigator has just landed in the New World."

Although the energy Fermi produced and cautiously controlled that day was only half a watt—enough to light a flashlight bulb—it was unique. By proving that a chain reaction could occur in a fissionable element, Fermi had taken mankind to the threshold of a great new source of power. It was now almost certain that atomic bombs could be built if enough U 235 or plutonium was secured. By making the greatest explosions ever known, they would assure victory for the Allies. In the more distant future, atomic energy, harnessed within reactors, would provide civilization with a multitude of important peacetime uses as yet scarcely dreamed of.

Fermi's accomplishment gave the green light to the "Manhattan District Project," the new code name for the uranium research and atomic bomb development. In the summer of 1942, the U. S. Army Corps of Engineers assumed control of both scientific work and the procurement and production of materials. Headed by General Leslie R. Groves, the program employed many scientists and military personnel and thousands of civilian workers, and eventually cost two billion dollars. In the deadly combat with Germany, the United States determined to succeed, no matter what cost or complications.

The story of the development of atomic energy illustrates the unpleasant axiom that strife among nations often advances technology, since practical applications are made of scientific knowledge that might otherwise remain unknown or ignored for years by all but a few specialists. Wanting to produce atomic bombs before the Nazis, our government supplied almost unlimited funds and enlisted the help of both military and American industrial know-how. The Manhattan District became Big Business.

Producing a chain reaction within an atomic pile was just the start of the actual construction of atomic bombs. A much smaller quantity of pure fissionable material would chain-react violently; but to obtain even miniscule amounts of the rare U 235 or of plutonium 239 involved complex industrial processes still mostly in the blueprint stage. At "Site X," a large tract of land at Oak Ridge, Tennessee, gigantic plants were built to separate U 235 from U 238—their first goal to produce just enough fissionable "enriched" uranium for a single, compact bomb. Yet few of the 75,000 employees at the huge Clinton Engineering Works knew what they were really making. They and the many other Americans who heard of this and other "secret cities" guessed wildly at the product being manufactured: a new kind of gasoline; a paint that made airplanes invisible; a death ray. And of course there were gags: they were producing FDR campaign buttons, or dehydrated water for overseas troops, or the front ends of sawhorses.

Alongside the Columbia River at Hanford, Washington, the DuPont Company built under government instructions three enormous nuclear reactors—the more sophisticated name for atomic piles or "furnaces"—in which tons of uranium ore would be converted into tiny amounts of plutonium 239. The third "secret city" was "Site Y," the mysterious, double-fence-enclosed community on a high, desolate mesa at Los Alamos, forty miles from Santa Fe, New Mexico. There, refugee scientists from Europe joined their American, English, and Canadian associates in designing the atomic bombs themselves, to be assembled as soon as enough fissionable material came from Oak Ridge and Hanford.

For a while the Fermis stayed on in Chicago. Enrico supervised the transfer of the atomic pile to the Argonne National Laboratory twenty miles away. He also made frequent trips to Oak Ridge, Hanford, and Los Alamos. When the atomic scientists traveled, they always had an alias and a bodyguard. Usually the assumed name kept the initials, if not the nationality, of the real one, and thus Enrico Fermi became "Eugene Farmer." (Once he was refused admittance at Oak Ridge because a suspicious guard decided that his swarthy complexion and Italian accent simply did not fit with "Farmer.") Enrico's bodyguard was an intelligent, amiable, and burly Italian-American named John Baudino, a peacetime lawyer drafted into the Counter Intelligence Corps. A born teacher, Fermi could not resist giving John an introductory course in nuclear physics. Baudino proved such a good pupil that he even learned to operate the Argonne reactor. Fermi often introduced him as "my colleague." And he would say, "Johnny knows too much. He's going to need a bodyguard."

The Fermis became United States citizens in 1944. In August they moved again—to Los Alamos. There Fermi served as an associate director, assisting J. Robert Oppenheimer. He was put in charge of the "F" (for Fermi) Division, which worked on the advanced design of the atomic bombs and also on theoretical problems, such as determining the "critical mass," the precise quantity of U 235 that would spontaneously explode when hit by a neutron.

Oppenheimer had originally envisaged Los Alamos as a small community of about a hundred people, but within several years its population was 6,000. Its residents were primarily scientists and engineers, who referred to each other, deprecatingly, as "eggheads" and "plumbers." Then there were the ever-present "creeps"—the C.I.C. men who tried to prevent absent-minded scientists from misplacing secret files or enthusiastically spouting in public about their work. So notorious were the scientists for their individual eccentricities that when General Groves first assembled his Los Alamos staff, he spoke bluntly: "At great expense on this mesa we have gathered together the largest collection of crackpots ever seen." And although Fermi considered himself utterly normal, even he cut an odd figure around the place, astride his bicycle with a battered blue hat and rolled-up pant legs.

At Los Alamos, hidden away from the eyes of the world, were many world-famous scientists (including four Nobel

Prize physicists). The neutron discoverer, James Chadwick, was there; and so was Niels Bohr, who had escaped from German-occupied Denmark in a fishing boat. All prominent scientists bore false names; scientific vocabulary did too. Atom became "top"; bomb was "boat," uranium "tube alloy," uranium fission "urchin fashion." When Laura Fermi took a part-time office job, she was baffled by the many strange words she encountered. Frequently loud bangs resounded around town, echoing up from the canyons where the scientists were testing detonating devices for the two types of bombs. Laura was scarcely reassured about the nature of her husband's work when Emilio Segré, a former member of Fermi's Roman physics group and now working on the bomb too, greeted her with, "Don't be afraid of becoming a widow. If Enrico blows up, you'll blow up too."

In the summer of 1945, the small but sufficient quantities of uranium 235 and plutonium 239 began to arrive. Like eager boys with new models to build, the scientists began constructing their bombs. The single uranium bomb, using a gun-type detonator, was almost sure to work, though with what explosive force was anybody's guess. The two plutonium bombs, with implosion mechanisms, were trickier devices that might not work at all; one bomb would have to be tested—which would also reveal the force of an atomic explosion.

The first atomic bomb test, given the code name of "Trinity," was scheduled for a pre-dawn hour on July 16, 1945, in the desert near the Alamogordo Air Base. The plutonium bomb, nicknamed "Fat Man," was placed on a steel structure a hundred feet above the ground, to be triggered by scientists in a dugout about five miles away. Ten miles away at the Base Camp the scientists and military personnel assembled to witness the test. To pass the time, the scientists started a gambling pool; each man put in a dollar and hazarded a guess as to the bomb's explosive yield. Some thought it might be equivalent only to a few tons of TNT; others suspected that their "firecracker" might not work at all. Meanwhile, to General Groves' annoyance, the puckish Enrico Fermi took side wagers on whether the bomb would destroy only New Mexico, or ignite the whole world's atmosphere. Later the General realized that this was simply Fermi's way of joking about the coming test, which was making almost everybody else nervous and somber.

On the night before the test the weather was wet. Some worried that lightning might set the bomb off prematurely. The test was postponed for several hours. Plans were made to evacuate nearby towns if radioactive fallout was spread by rain or wind. An official bulletin had already been prepared to give to any reporters hearing of a surprisingly big bang: it told of an accidental explosion of an ammunition magazine at Alamogordo Air Base.

When the weather somewhat improved, Dr. Oppenheimer and General Groves decided to take a chance and set zero hour for 5:30 A.M. As the countdown began, the men in the observation dugouts were instructed to lie face-down with their feet pointing toward the blast. Right on schedule, "Fat Man" exploded—with the incredible brightness of a man-made sun shattering earth and air. Within a few seconds a gigantic fireball in the now-familiar mushroom shape was climbing toward the sky.

The scientists jumped to their feet. Some shouted, danced, and shook hands. Others stood silent and shaken, now fully aware that they had contrived no toy, no mere firecracker, but a weapon that could ultimately destroy the world. Waiting for the shock wave he knew would come less than a minute after the explosion, Fermi began to dribble bits of paper to the ground. (A young engineer watching him decided that the bomb had knocked Fermi "clear off his rocker.") In fifty seconds the roar came, with a sudden swift wind that blew the paper bits several feet away before they dropped. After measuring the distance they had traveled, Fermi told the other men that the blast had been equivalent to 20,000 tons of TNT—the highest figure optimists had chosen but had really not expected to realize. Always liking to work on mathematical puzzles, especially to find short-cut solutions, Fermi had calculated in advance for various explosive yields exactly how far the paper pieces would go at the instant the shock wave hit. By this simple experiment he got the same figure recorded by complex devices closer to the bomb.

An hour later Fermi climbed into a lead-lined tank to explore the site of the explosion. What he saw made a grim testament to the bomb's destructive power. A wide crater had been dug in the desert floor, and within a mile of the desolate site there was not a sign of life—animal or vegetable. The tremendous heat of the blast had fused the sand into shimmering green-glass particles. Returning to Base Camp, Fermi found that his usual calm had fled; he asked a friend to drive his car during the trip back to Los Alamos.

The Trinity test was an unqualified success. But it now posed one of the most difficult questions of all time: should the United States drop the two other atomic bombs, on their way to the Pacific, on Japan? For months military people, high government leaders, and scientists had debated the issue. With Leo Szilard as their spokesman, some scientists asserted that the atomic bombs should not be used at all; or if they were used, the first one should not fall on any human target but instead should provide a warning demonstration before Japanese witnesses.

President Truman, who had learned of the bombs' existence only after he became President following Roosevelt's recent death, appointed an Interim Committee to study the various arguments for and against the use of atomic bombs; Fermi was selected as one of the four scientist-advisers. The panel concluded that the only effective solution was to use the two available bombs on cities, so that the Japanese people themselves would fully recognize the futility of continuing the war, which they might otherwise fight to a suicidal finish, involving the invasion of the mainland islands and the probable loss of hundreds of thousands of American lives.

Three weeks after Trinity, the uranium and plutonium bombs were dropped on Hiroshima and Nagasaki, and the Second World War was swiftly over. No longer a well-kept secret was the dramatic work of Manhattan District. All in a rush, newspapers and magazines, which had been forbidden even to use the word "atom" during the war years, told of the making of the atomic bombs. And prominent among the story's heroes was the "Italian Navigator," Enrico Fermi. His contribution especially pleased those Italian-Americans whose loyalty had been questioned during the past years.

His bomb work over, Fermi left Los Alamos at the end of 1945. He was glad to return to pure research in a university atmosphere away from barbed wire, aliases, and military watchdogs. His family settled once more in Chicago, where Fermi started work at the new Institute for Basic Research connected with the University of Chicago. He returned at first to his specialty, the neutron. When a huge cyclotron was built at the University of Chicago, making it possible for scientists to create little-known atomic particles like mesons, Fermi switched to studying fundamental particles and cosmic rays.

On March 19, 1946, Enrico Fermi received the Congressional Medal of Merit, the highest award accorded to civilians, which was presented to him by General Groves. "To Enrico Fermi for exceptionally meritorious conduct in the performance of outstanding service to the War Department," his citation read, in part. "A great experimental physicist, Dr. Fermi's sound scientific judgment, his initiative and resourcefulness, and his unswerving devotion to duty have contributed vitally to the success of the Atomic Bomb project."

Fermi had unlocked a double door to the Atomic Age: one door led to terrible death and destruction in time of war, the other to limitless benefits for mankind in peacetime. For several years Fermi served on the General Advisory Committee of the Atomic Energy Commission, the government agency created to direct further nuclear research. For defense purposes the AEC was developing other nuclear weapons, like the thermonuclear, fusion-type bomb—far more powerful than the atomic bomb. But the AEC also initiated many constructive uses for atomic power. In nuclear reactors long-lasting radioisotopes like cobalt 60 were inexpensively created, giving universities and hospitals their own sources for radiation. Radioisotopes could be used in medicine to diagnose and treat diseases, in biological research, agriculture, and industry in an ever-expanding variety of ways. Atomic energy was also adapted as a fuel for ships and for producing electricity. Meanwhile, scientists found more man-made elements. Element 100 was named Fermium to honor Enrico Fermi.

A brilliant and inspiring lecturer, Dr. Fermi was sought

by many universities throughout the United States and Europe. In the summer of 1952, he gave talks at several schools of advanced physics in France and Italy. Although his mind was as keen as ever, he seemed to lack his usual physical exuberance. On his return to Chicago, it became known that Fermi was suffering from cancer, a malady often afflicting those who have worked closely with radioactive materials.

In early November of 1954, Enrico Fermi received the Atomic Energy Commission's first award for "especially meritorious contributions for the development, use, or control of atomic energy"—an annual prize known today as the Enrico Fermi Award. Several weeks later, on November 28, Fermi died.

"There is no doubt among those who knew him and could appreciate his accomplishments," said Samuel K. Allison in a farewell tribute, "that Enrico Fermi was one of the most brilliant intellects of our century. Here was a man who possessed a most extraordinary endowment of the highest human capabilities."

This century's Italian navigator had departed prematurely for the dark shores of yet another world.

A Summing Up

The Italians Stay

"You dreamed dreams of what America was to be. . . .
Just because you brought dreams with you, America is
more likely to realize dreams such as you brought."

IN ALL OCCUPATIONS in the United States, Italian-Americans
are apt to be found. Every American community may have
men of Italian ancestry who are street cleaners, construction
workers, and shoe repairmen. And there also will be people
with Italian names who are teachers, lawyers, doctors.

Like the other immigrant groups in our country, the
Italians have done their share of work—and more. Italian-
Americans play in major orchestras, win football and baseball games for their college or professional teams, or entertain
millions of other Americans by performing in movies, on
stage, or in television. They are artists, university professors,
scientists, journalists, politicians, clergymen, judges.

Italian-Americans help to feed us by growing our produce,
manufacturing our foodstuffs, or shipping them; they operate
grocery stores; they own or staff restaurants across the nation.
People of Italian descent design buildings, furniture, cars,

rugs, and books; they chart the courses of industrial or financial empires; they assist in launching rockets into space; as scientists they probe the mysteries of life and of the universe. Men with Italian surnames occupy town halls, governors' mansions, and the legislatures and supreme courts of states; they sit in the Senate and in the House of Representatives. Someday, doubtless a President of the United States will have a recognizably Italian-American background.

The longer Italians stay among us, the better able we are to recognize their worth. Increasingly now, they are in second and third generations removed from Italy; some may be of pure Italian stock, others may be only one-half or one-quarter Italian. Most are as genuinely American as anyone whose ancestors came over on the *Mayflower*. Yet often a component remains in them to remind them and others of an Italian ancestral origin: some Italian traits seem durable, not likely to fade quickly away. In Italian-Americans one usually notices a zest for life itself; a deep love and loyalty for family; pleasure in food, companionship, laughter; robust and honest emotions; gestures that speak as eloquently as the tongue; a real liking for work, whether manual or cerebral.

Partly because Italians live and work among us we have become what we are. Probably the best-known Italians in America have worked in the performing arts. When Lorenzo Da Ponte, the librettist for Mozart's *Don Giovanni*, brought an Italian opera company to New York in 1832, he started the popularity of Italian opera in America. During the nineteenth century, Italian singers like Adelina Patti got such a warm reception in America that they and their successors came regularly, to give concerts and appear with American opera groups. Often their engagements are so prolonged that they establish permanent residences in the United States and sometimes they become citizens. Among the notable Italian singers of the past have been that incomparable tenor, Enrico Caruso, and also Giovanni Martinelli, Tito Schipa, Beniamino Gigli, Amelita Galli-Curci, Licia Albanese, Ezio Pinza. More recently to our shores have come Renata Tebaldi, Mario del Monaco, Franco Corelli, Giorgio Tozzi, Cesare Siepi, Giulietta Simionato. Many opera singers have also been American-born of Italian descent: Rosa and Carmela Ponselle, Dusolina Giannini, Richard Bonelli, Robert Merrill, and Vivian Della Chiesa. (An Italian surname once seemed so much an asset in pursuing an opera career that non-Italian singers sometimes assumed Italian surnames—an ironic contrast to the tendency among some Italian-Americans to shorten or alter their names, either for easier pronunciation or to disguise an origin in some scorned "Little Italy.")

Italian-American singers of popular music have been even better known to the American public. Among them are Frank Sinatra, Perry Como, Dean Martin, Tony Bennett, Frankie Laine, Vic Damone, Mario Lanza, and Connie Francis. Anna Maria Alberghetti, born in Italy, has become an American citizen. Sergio Franchi, who sings romantic songs in both Italian and English, has had great success in the United States. Performing in the same area, Eddie Duchin was a highly popular pianist and band leader; his son, Peter Duchin, follows in his footsteps. Other "swing" orchestra leaders of Italian background have been Guy Lombardo, Frankie Carle, Carmen Cavallero, and Louis Prima.

In classical music Italians and Italian-Americans have thrived. Two of the first music conservatories in America were founded in Boston and Philadelphia in the early 1800s by the Italian musician and composer Philip Traetta—a friend of the presidents Madison and Monroe. Since the playing of music in the home was encouraged by many

Italian families, it is no surprise that many Italian-Americans found careers in music, as conductors, instrumentalists, arrangers, or instructors. Six of the conductors of the famed U. S. Marine Corps Band have been Italian. One of the best-known Italian-American virtuoso instrumentalists is violinist Ruggiero Ricci.

Italian-Americans also compose music—those most familiar to Americans being Walter Piston, Norman Dello Joio, and Gian-Carlo Menotti. The Italian-born Menotti writes both music and libretto for his modern operas, which include *Amahl and the Night Visitors, The Medium, The Telephone,* and *The Saint of Bleecker Street.* Working in a lighter vein is the Hollywood composer Henry Mancini and many other Italian-Americans composing popular songs.

The acting profession has long known Italians. Italy has a rich history of drama, and some of her greatest actors—Tommaso Salvini, Adelaide Ristori, Eleonora Duse—visited the United States. By now most Americans associate the Italians in their midst with the theatrical arts as much as they do with the world of music. An early nation-wide movie idol was the Italian-born Rudolph Valentino (who, oddly enough, fluttered hearts during the 1920s, when prejudice against Italians was at its peak). Don Ameche was a perennial favorite as a movie actor; well-known character actors have been Henry Armetta, Eduardo Cianelli, Joseph Callea, and Monty Banks. The handsome, basso-voiced opera star Ezio Pinza, leaving the Metropolitan Opera to appear in the stage musicals *South Pacific* and *Fanny* and also in several movies, acquired many new admirers. The stage singer-actor Alfred Drake is of Italian descent. Singers Frank Sinatra and Dean Martin have established great secondary successes as movie actors.

Nowadays many actors shuttle between New York and

Hollywood—performing on stage, making movies, appearing in television roles; among contemporary actors of Italian ancestry are Ernest Borgnine, Anthony Franciosa, Ben Gazzara, and Anne Bancroft (born Anna Italiano). The increasingly international film business has made Italian stars like Sophia Loren, Gina Lollobrigida, Rossano Brazzi, Vittorio Gassman, and Marcello Mastroianni as popular among Americans as their own movie actors.

From the *commedia dell' arte* days of sixteenth-century Italy, Italian performers have shown a knack for arousing laughter. Notable Italian-American comedians have been Jimmy Savo, Lou Costello, Jerry Colonna, and Jimmy Durante. Using puppets in the marionette theatre, Remo Bufano long entertained audiences. In the entertainment business Italian-Americans also function behind the scenes as producers, impresarios, directors, writers, set and costume designers, choreographers, and camera men. (Two famous Italian-American movie directors are Frank Capra and Vincente Minelli.)

In the fine arts Italian-Americans have also done very well, partly because Italians already had a strong tradition of accomplishment in painting, sculpture, and architecture—so art as a career possibility was comprehended and usually encouraged in the Italian home. Italian immigrants had often worked as stonecutters in marble quarries or cemeteries; in the cities, skilled but lowly sculptors might shape little plaster statues of saints or popular leaders, tint them, and sell them in the streets. Frequently their children became sculptors of public statuary and embellishments for buildings. Many sculptors working in America came originally from Italy, the most famous perhaps being Attilio Piccirilli, who worked on monuments for both New York and Washington, D.C. The Rome-born sculptor Beniamino Bufano has contributed a number of ingenuous and unique sculptures to the San Francisco area, most notably his statue of Peace at the entrance to the International Airport.

Italians in America have been portraitists, muralists, and landscape artists since Colonial days. The Italian-born painter Rico Lebrun is probably the best-known modern artist among Italian-Americans. By applying art to commerce many have succeeded as illustrators and graphic designers. Italian artists who have written and illustrated children's books, some of them considered classics, are Valenti Angelo, Leo Politi, and Leo Lionni. A list of the art directors in advertising agencies and large corporations will have a disproportionate number of Italian names. The field of architecture too attracts many Italian-Americans: two prominent ones are Anthony J. DePace and Pietro Belluschi, head of the Department of Architecture at M.I.T. Surely a magnificent curiosity in America "folk" art and architecture are the lacy, spiral towers made of steel and concrete, decorated with mosaics, built in the Watts section of Los Angeles by the immigrant Simon Rodia to celebrate his residence in America; they have been designated a Cultural Heritage Monument. In Arizona, Paolo Soleri makes unusual ceramics, and is acquiring an important reputation as a futuristic designer of cities.

In sports—a corner of the entertainment world—Italian-Americans have contributed handsomely. Their first notable success came in prize fighting, inevitably an arena where pugilists of "second class" nationality or race have made their mark—and sometimes a good deal of money as well. Among the early title holders were Sam and Vince Lazzaro, brothers using the names Joe and Vince Dundee, who became welterweight and middleweight champions. Ranking with the great boxers of all time is Rocky Marciano, who retired undefeated as heavyweight champion of the world. A boy from Massachusetts, in his years in the ring he earned over four million dollars—the largest fortune ever made by a fighter.

The records of two uniquely American sports, baseball and football, are studded with Italian names. Italian-Americans as a group got a late start; so many of them grew up in crowded city sections, where streets provided little room for field sports and large parks were far away. Also, a talented young ballplayer rarely received parental approval in pursuing a professional career in sports: they would often be told that instead of spending their time foolishly, throwing balls around, they should go out and get a useful job. The lucrative aspect of turning mere boys' "play" into a highly skilled, well-paying profession was inconceivable. Nowadays, of course, the attitude has wholly changed, as more and more Italian-Americans enter and excel at sports. Among the famed baseball players are Joe Di Maggio, Phil Rizzuto, and Yogi Berra—all perennial stars for the Yankees. Two prominent football players were Frank Carideo and Joe Savoldi of Notre Dame. Other sports favored by Italian-Americans are golf, automobile racing, and horse racing.

Two principal features of Italian life—food and wine—have employed many Italians in America. Since many grew up in farm areas, Italians understood and liked working with produce. Some were able to buy truck farms in America, where they grew vegetables and fruits so successfully that they expanded their enterprises, a few becoming great landowners. Others served as shippers or wholesalers for produce, or as merchants. "Patsy" D'Agostino of New York gradually built up a chain of grocery stores and a considerable fortune.

Still others began the manufacture in America of Italian foodstuffs. Among the pasta makers, Buitoni and La Rosa have begun producing other kinds of foods as well.

Much of the growth and vigor of the American wine industry can be traced to Italians, both as wine makers and as consumers. Italian-Swiss Colony was originally started in 1881 as a cooperative agricultural colony in Napa Valley. Many of the small or medium-sized "quality" vineyards in California were planted or revived following the Prohibition era by Italian-Americans. Fine wines are made by Louis Martini and by the Mondavi family of Charles Krug Winery. Italian big-businessmen holding huge vineyard estates—like Petri and the Gallo brothers—have popularized the drinking of wine in the United States through extensive advertising; by modern production and merchandising methods they produce inexpensive wines in vast quantities.

In other business enterprises too, Italians have noticeably succeeded. When unskilled workers from southern Italy and Sicily poured into America around the turn of the century, to mine ores, build cities, and span the continent with transportation and communication lines, most of them worked as lowly day laborers—or at best as *padroni,* the labor agents, gang bosses, or overseers for those who could not speak English and could not fend for themselves. Gradually, the more ambitious Italians rose to higher positions and often started construction businesses of their own. The first Italian-American to become a millionaire was Generoso Pope, who as a young immigrant worked as a waterboy on a road gang. Later he bought sand and gravel pits, ran a contracting business, then branched out into a complex string of business projects—one of which was the publication of the influential *Il Progresso Italo-Americano* of New York, the nation's most

widely read Italian-American newspaper. His son Fortunato
Pope continues his enterprises. Other Italians, starting out
as steamship-company agents who also handled immigrants'
affairs—their savings, sending money back home to their
families, writing letters—formed immigrants' banks, some of
which developed into full-fledged banks, and usually were
leaders in Italian communities.

Many Italian-Americans became lawyers—a good proportion starting out by rendering legal services to the big-city
Italian colonies. Probably the best-known trial lawyer today
of Italian ancestry is Melvin Belli, the "king of torts." As
more and more Italians became naturalized citizens, and as
their children reached voting age, the Italian urban vote
was sought by political parties, who generally chose Italian-
Americans to run in heavily Italian districts. So Italian-
Americans, usually trained as lawyers, entered politics and
often gained from the Italian vote bloc a post in the city or
state government, a judgeship, or even a seat in Congress.
Frequently the office-holder stuck closely to the interests of
his constituents while toeing the party line; but sometimes,
as with Congressmen Fiorello La Guardia and Vito Marcantonio, and elective judges like Ferdinand Pecora and
Salvatore Cotillo, they were conscientious leaders concerned
about the well-being of all Americans. The Italian-American
La Guardia, as Congressman and mayor of New York City,
started out as something of an oddity politically. But partly
because of his success, and partly because times changed
rapidly, Italians became front-runners in politics: in 1949,
the four major contenders for the New York mayoralty were
Italian-Americans—Edward Corsi (a former Commissioner of
Immigration), Ferdinand Pecora, Vito Marcantonio, and—
the winner—Vincent Impelliteri.

Italian politicians also forged ahead across the nation, especially in the Northeastern states and on the West Coast. Angelo Rossi was one of San Francisco's most popular mayors. For years Alberto Rosselini served as governor of Washington state. Other state governors have been Massachusetts's Foster Furcolo and John Volpe, New York's Charles Poletti, Ohio's Michael V. Di Salle, Rhode Island's John A. Notte and John O. Pastore. Pastore, an eloquent orator and skillful political tactician, later became a Senator—the highest elective office yet achieved by anyone of Italian lineage. During the past decades the House of Representatives has had many Italian-Americans serving there. The highest appointive office held up to now by someone of Italian ancestry was the cabinet post of Secretary of Health, Education, and Welfare, to which President Kennedy appointed Anthony J. Celebrezze, the former reform mayor of Cleveland. A close aide to President Johnson was Jack Valenti, who in 1966 resigned to become the highly paid president of the Motion Picture Association of America.

Affiliated with politics for years have been the trade unions. The Italians were slow in uniting to improve their working lot. At first usually desperate for work at any wage under any conditions, regrettably they sometimes served as "scab" or strike-breaking labor during long strikes by the early unions, which subsequently gave Italians a bad reputation as a labor group with union leaders and members. However, as the Italians stayed on in America, their understanding of the gross exploitation of their labor increased; inevitably, some of their midst came forward to be labor union leaders. Among the best-known are Luigi Antonini of the International Ladies Garment Union, August Bellanca of the

Amalgamated Clothing Workers of America, and James C. Petrillo of the American Federation of Musicians.

Not all Italian-Americans have necessarily worked for the public good. For a few decades many Americans automatically associated Italians with the criminal elements in society, in part because of the notoriety of criminals like Al Capone and "Lucky" Luciano, constantly maintained through the stereotyped presentation of Italian-American gangsters in movies and in television series (to which groups like the Sons of Italy in America effectively protested). The Mafia, the Black Hand, the Camorra, and Cosa Nostra: these are names for various organized crime syndicates in which Italian names have predominated.

The original Mafia started in Sicily, where, dominated for centuries by rapacious rulers, the people had scant respect for laws or for government agents imposing them. Ruthless, unethical individuals desiring power and easy money banded together to threaten the rest of the populace with a variety of terrors if they did not pay "protection" or do as bidden. In the flood of Sicilian and southern Italian immigrants to America, inevitably some Mafia-type leaders and their cohorts came too. City police departments and the F.B.I. (itself founded by an Italian-American named Charles J. Bonaparte) often assigned Italian-American agents to snare Italian gangsters: the most famous among them was the police hero Giuseppe Petrosino.

Because Italian-American lawbreakers usually did things with a dramatic flair, because their names were distinctively Italian, because they joined together in strong organizations, and because they were good businessmen (crime can be a business too), they were noticed by other Americans, who believed their crimes to be out of proportion to their numbers. Sociological studies in recent decades have displayed statistically that the Italian-Americans commit no more crimes than any other nationality groups in the United States; some surveys acually show a crime rate lower than that of native American stock. (Other statistics relating to the Italians in America showed an exceedingly low rate, compared to most other groups, of drunkenness, pauperism, and hospital charity cases.)

Also in the "black book" of Italian names in the United States are two prominent ones: Nicola Sacco and Bartolomeo Vanzetti. The two Italian-born anarchists were convicted of taking part in a robbery and murder at a factory in Braintree, Massachusetts, in 1921. Probably no other legal case in American history has aroused such divided feelings within our nation. The Sacco-Vanzetti trial became a *cause célèbre* for liberal Americans, who believed that the conviction had been influenced by the men's reputation as radicals and by the prejudice of the court and state officials. Many maintained that the two defendants were being persecuted and prosecuted not for any actual crime, but because they represented a maligned minority group and were also political agitators. To their many fervid, loyal defenders throughout the Western world, Sacco and Vanzetti became sainted martyrs. In the succession of heated public debates, trials, and case reviews—ending with the execution of the men in 1927—few people, if any, were able to obtain a completely objective view of the situation's facts. Since the truth may never be known, even today speculation as to the men's innocence or guilt continues.

As a counterweight to such notoriety, the loyalty of other Italian immigrants to their adopted country, or that of their descendants, has been proven innumerable times during wartime. Francisco Vigo, a successful fur trader, became a patriot during the Revolutionary War when he joined with George Rogers Clark to keep the British forces from the western frontier. During the Civil War many Italians served the Union as both officers and enlisted men. (Lincoln actually offered a general's rank to the Italian soldier-hero Garibaldi, but it was declined.) In both world wars Italian-American servicemen earned high military honors. One of the most praised heroes of World War II was Marine Sergeant John Basilone, whom General MacArthur called a "one-man army"; he received the Congressional Medal of Honor and, posthumously, the Navy Cross.

Americans hearing of Enrico Fermi's part in developing the atomic bomb began to notice that Italians had been working among them for years in the fields of science, engineering, medicine, and education. Young Italian immigrants easily adapting themselves to America, as well as second- and third-generation Italian-Americans, had made good use of new educational opportunities and unrestricted futures in expanding technological fields. Basically a practical people, Italians have often been more inclined toward the application of science to industry and human needs, rather than toward pure or theoretical research. The nineteenth-century inventor Antonio Meucci is frequently credited with the invention of the first telephone, ahead of Alexander Graham Bell. An Italian-American horticulturist named E. O. Fenzi experimented for twenty years in introducing plants from all over the world to the warm climate and rich soil of California. Electricity experts Peter Bellaschi and Giuseppe Faccioli were chief engineers for years at Westinghouse and General Electric. Giuseppe Bellanca, a pioneer aviator, was a noted airplane designer.

In the natural and physical sciences there are and have been many Italian-Americans—on the faculties of universities, or working on research in industries and in government service. In the medical world many skilled, dedicated physicians have had Italian names, one of the most famous being William Francis Verdi of the Yale University Medical School.

The Italians in America have been noteworthy educators. The first Italian professor here probably was Mazzei's and Jefferson's friend Carlo Bellini, who was Professor of Romance Languages at William and Mary College. During the nineteenth century many well-educated Italians came to America to teach. Another influx came beginning in the 1930s, when large numbers of Italian intellectuals fled Fascist rule in their homeland and were welcomed by American universities. Columbia University started Casa Italiana in the 1920s, a school that specialized in the study of the Italian language and culture, and as a sideline encouraged interest in Italian-American accomplishments. Among well-known Italian-American educators have been Mario Pei of Columbia University, one of the world's foremost linguistic authorities; the psychologist Leonard Covello; the sociologist Constantine Panunzio; and Angelo Patri, a New York City high-school principal who wrote many popular books on child training as well as a nationally syndicated newspaper column.

Closely connected with education and social service are the many Italian-American clergymen and members of religious orders. Ever since the early settlement of the country, Italian priests took prominent places in American life, at first as missionaries, explorers, and colonists' leaders (notably Father Eusabio Chino—or Kino—in the Southwest), then as educators. A brilliant, highly versatile priest of the nineteenth century was Benedict Sestini from Rome, who in his busy career was a professor of mathematics, astronomy, and geology as well as a church architect and the founder-editor of the popular Catholic magazine (which continues today), *Messenger of the Sacred Heart.* Priests and nuns from Italy were especially helpful in the years of the heavy Italian immigration by teaching at parochial schools that bridged the Old and New World cultures. Today, a good portion of the American-born Roman Catholic clergy is of Italian stock. Although the majority of Italians have been raised in the Catholic faith, some were brought up as, or became, Protestants; among them have been ministers who worked in the Italian colonies in churches and in settlement houses.

Since Italian tradition encouraged girls to stay at home, becoming wives and mothers, Italian-American women usually did not pursue at first the variety of careers that attracted their brothers, except in unique places where females were necessary—such as opera singing. Many Italian women, however, did add to the family income by taking in boarders, sewing, and making hats and artificial flowers. Nowadays, more and more Italian-American women are entering the fields of business, education, the applied arts, and science.

Through the writings of Italian-Americans themselves, the Italian experience in America is most fully and intimately seen. These books and stories express in personal and human terms, not as statistics or case histories, the struggles of the people themselves to blend the values and memories of the homeland with the challenges and opportunities of America. Probably the most moving account of the Italian "pick-and-shovel" immigrant's life is the poet Pascal D'Angelo's autobiography, *Son of Italy.* Another interesting account of the American encounter was told by Constantine Panunzio in *The Soul of an Immigrant.* A popular novel of an immigrant's life is Pietro Di Donato's *Christ in Concrete*. Other good Italian-American fiction has been written by Jerre Mangione, Michael Capite, John Fante, Guido D'Agostino, and Jo Pagano. Two excellent books were by Angelo Pellegrini, Professor of English at the University of Washington: his autobiography, *Immigrant's Return,* and an equally fascinating study of six Italian-American lives, *Americans by Choice.*

Well-known writers of full or partial Italian ancestry are Paul Gallico, Hamilton Basso, John Ciardi, and Bernard De Voto. Three Italian-born writers who settled in the United States are editor Max Ascoli, Laura (Mrs. Aldous) Huxley, and novelist-biographer Frances Winwar (pseudonym-translation for Francesca Vinceguerra).

Just as the nine subjects of this book were distinct individuals who affected, and were affected by, America, so were all of the nearly five million Italians who came to our nation during the past centuries, each with a dream of his own. "You dreamed dreams of what America was to be," said President Woodrow Wilson when he addressed a group of new citizens, "and I hope you brought the dreams with you. No man that does not see visions will ever realize any high hope or undertake any high enterprise. Just because you brought dreams with you, America is more likely to realize dreams such as you brought. You are enriching us if you came expecting us to be better than we are." And the way to achieve those dreams, Wilson said, was by working. "We cannot exempt you from work," he said. "We cannot exempt you from the strife and the heartbreaking burden of the struggle of the day—that is common to mankind everywhere; we cannot exempt you from the loads you must carry. We can only make them light by the spirit in which they are carried. That is the spirit of hope, it is the spirit of liberty, it is the spirit of justice."

Sometimes the ideal spirits which the President outlined were but rarely glimpsed in America by the immigrant, but still they were there as he toiled, making some mark upon the new land—perhaps only something hardly noticeable or transitory . . . but made nevertheless. Some newcomers thrived, some just got by, and some failed; in each immigrant's life a separate vision of America developed. But whatever his experience, he usually stayed and had children, who had children too—all of them born as American citizens. His memory of his beloved homeland faded, but he cherished and idealized what he remembered. To his children, however, Italy was just the ancestral place; home was America. His legacy to them might only have consisted of American citizenship; but it was all they needed to move ahead and follow their own dreams, often to succeed as their parents sometimes could not.

They live and work among us now as Americans. The Italians have come to stay. They are sturdy, bright-hued threads woven firmly and irremovably in the fabric of America.

Bibliography

THE ITALIAN BACKGROUND

Barzini, Luigi. *The Italians*. New York: Atheneum (1964).

Burckhardt, Jakob. *The Civilization of the Renaissance in Italy*. London: Phaidon Press (1937).

Fermi, Laura. *Mussolini*. Chicago: University of Chicago Press (1961).

Hibbert, Christopher. *Garibaldi and His Enemies*. Boston: Little, Brown (1966).

Kubly, Herbert. *American in Italy*. New York: Simon & Schuster (1954).

Levine, Irving R. *Main Street, Italy*. New York: Doubleday (1963).

Morton, H. V. *A Traveller in Italy*. New York: Dodd, Mead (1965).

Pei, Mario. *The Story of Language*. Philadelphia: J. B. Lippincott (1949).

Phillips, John. *Face of a Nation: The Italians*. New York: McGraw-Hill (1965).

Sforza, Count Carlo. *Italy and Italians*. New York: E. P. Dutton (1949).

Smith, Denis M. *Italy*. Ann Arbor, Mich.: University of Michigan Press (1959).

Trevelyan, Janet Penrose. *A Short History of the Italian People*. New York: G. P. Putnam's Sons (1920).

IMMIGRANTS AND IMMIGRATION

Adamic, Louis. *A Nation of Nations*. New York: Harper & Bros. (1945).

Bennett, Marion T. *American Immigration Policies*. Washington, D. C.: Public Affairs Press (1963).

Bowers, David F. (editor). *Foreign Influences in American Life*. New York: Peter Smith (1952).

Fairchild, Henry Pratt. *Immigration: A World Movement and Its American Significance*. New York: Macmillan (1925).

Gateway to Citizenship. Pamphlet prepared by United States Department of Justice, Immigration and Naturalization Service. Washington, D. C.: U. S. Government Printing Office (revised edition, 1962).

Glazer, Nathan, and Moynihan, Daniel P. *Beyond the Melting Pot.* Cambridge, Mass.: M. I. T. and Harvard University Press (1963).

Grant, Madison. *The Passing of the Great Race.* New York: Charles Scribner's Sons (1922).

Handlin, Oscar (editor). *Children of the Uprooted.* New York: George Braziller (1966).

———. *Immigration as a Factor in American History.* Englewood Cliffs, New Jersey: Prentice-Hall (1959).

Handlin, Oscar. *The Uprooted.* Boston: Little, Brown (1951).

Hansen, Marcus Lee. *The Immigrant in American History.* Cambridge, Mass.: Harvard University Press (1940).

Kennedy, John F. *A Nation of Immigrants.* New York: Harper & Row (1964).

Panunzio, Constantine. *Immigration Crossroads.* New York: Macmillan (1927).

Seabrook, William. *These Foreigners.* New York: Harcourt, Brace (1938).

Smith, William Carlson. *Americans in the Making.* New York: Appleton-Century (1939).

Steiner, Edward A. *On the Trail of the Immigrant.* New York: Fleming H. Revell (1906).

THE ITALIANS IN AMERICA

Child, Irvin L. *Italian or American?—The Second Generation in Conflict.* New Haven, Conn.: Yale University Press (1943).

Curinga, Nicola. *An Italian Tragedy: The Story of a Humble People.* New York: Liveright (1945).

Foerster, Robert F. *Italian Emigration of Our Times.* Cambridge, Mass.: Harvard University Press (1919).

Guidi, Angelo F. *Italy and the Italians in Washington's Time.* New York: Italian Publishers (1933).

Italian-American Who's Who. (In twenty editions.) New York: Vigo Press.

Lord, Eliot, et al. *The Italian in America.* New York: B. F. Buck (1905).

Mangano, Antonio. *Sons of Italy.* New York: Methodist Book Concern (1917).

Marraro, Howard R. *American Opinion on the Unification of Italy, 1846-1861.* New York: Columbia University Press (1932).

Musmanno, Michael A. *The Story of the Italians in America.* New York: Doubleday & Co. (1965).

Pergallo, Olga. *Italian-American Authors and Their Contribution to American Literature.* New York: S. F. Vanni (1949).

Pisani, Lawrence Frank. *The Italian in America.* New York: Exposition Press (1957).

Rose, Philip M. *The Italians in America.* New York: George H. Doran (1922).

Sartorio, Enrico. *Social and Religious Life of Italians in America.* Boston: Christopher Publishing House (1918).

Schiavo, Giovanni. *Four Centuries of Italian-American History.* New York: Vigo Press (1957).

——. *The Italians in America Before the Civil War.* New York: Vigo Press (1934).

Stella, Antonio. *Italian Immigration to the United States.* New York: G. P. Putnam's Sons (1924).

Turano, Anthony M. "The Speech of Little Italy," *American Mercury,* July 1932.

Whyte, William F. *Street-Corner Society: The Social Structure of an Italian Slum.* Chicago: University of Chicago Press (revised edition 1955).

Williams, Phyllis H. *South Italian Folkways in Europe and America.* New Haven: Yale University Press (1938).

WPA. *The Italians of New York: A Survey.* New York: Random House (1938).

ITALIAN-AMERICAN AUTOBIOGRAPHIES AND BIOGRAPHIES

Caruso, Dorothy. *Enrico Caruso: His Life and Death.* New York: Simon & Schuster (1945).

Corsi, Edward. *In the Shadow of Liberty.* New York: Macmillan (1935).

Covello, Leonard. (With Guido D'Agostino.) *The Heart Is the Teacher.* New York: McGraw-Hill (1958).

D'Angelo, Pascal. *Son of Italy.* New York: Macmillan (1924).

Ferber, Nat. *A New American: The Story of Justice Salvatore A. Cotillo.* New York: Farrar & Rinehart (1938).

Graziano, Rocky. (With Rowland Barber.) *Somebody Up There Likes Me.* New York: Simon & Schuster (1954).

Musmanno, Michael A. *Verdict: The Adventures of the Young Lawyer in the Brown Suit.* New York: Doubleday (1958).

Panunzio, Constantine. *The Soul of an Immigrant.* New York: Macmillan (1937).

Patri, Angelo. *A Schoolmaster of the Great City.* New York. Macmillan (1928).

Pellegrini, Angelo M. *Americans by Choice.* New York: Macmillan (1956).

——. *Immigrant's Return.* New York: Macmillan (1952).

Pinza, Ezio. *Ezio Pinza: An Autobiography*. (With Robert Magidoff.) New York: Rinehart (1958).

Russell, Francis. *Tragedy in Dedham: The Story of the Sacco-Vanzetti Case*. New York: McGraw-Hill (1962).

Ventresca, Francesco. *Personal Reminiscences of a Naturalized American*. New York: Daniel Ryerson (1937).

Villa, Silvio. *The Unbidden Guest*. New York: Macmillan (1922).

HENRI DE TONTI

Brebner, John Bartlett. *The Explorers of North America*. New York: Macmillan (1933).

Cuthbertson, George A. *Freshwater: A History and Narrative of the Great Lakes*. New York: Macmillan (1931).

Davis, Edwin Adams. *Louisiana, the Pelican State*. Baton Rouge: Louisiana State University Press (1959).

Finley, John. *The French in the Heart of America*. New York: Charles Scribner's Sons (1915).

Gray, James. *The Illinois*. New York: Farrar & Rinehart (1940).

Havighurst, Walter. *The Heartland: Ohio, Indiana, Illinois*. New York: Harper & Row (1962).

———. *The Long Ships Passing*. New York: Macmillan (1942).

Kellogg, Louise P. (editor). *Early Narratives of the Northwest, 1634-1699*. (For "Memoir on La Salle's Discoveries, by Tonty" and "The Voyage of St. Cosme, 1698-1699.") New York: Barnes and Noble (reprinted 1959).

Murphy, Edmund R. *Henry de Tonty, Fur Trader of the Mississippi*. Baltimore: Johns Hopkins Press (1941).

Parish, J. C. *The Man with the Iron Hand*. Chicago (1913).

Parkman, Francis. *La Salle and the Discovery of the Great West*. Boston: Little, Brown (1896).

Reed, C. B. *Masters of the Wilderness*. Boston (1913).

PHILIP MAZZEI

Bowers, Claude. *The Young Jefferson*. Boston: Houghton Mifflin (1945).

Boyd, Julian P. (editor). *The Papers of Thomas Jefferson*. New Jersey: Princeton University Press (1952-   ).

Garlick, Jr., Richard C. *Philip Mazzei, Friend of Jefferson: His Life and Letters*. Baltimore, Md.: Johns Hopkins Press (1933).

Marraro, Howard R. (editor). *Unpublished Mazzei Letters to Jefferson*. William and Mary Quarterly, 3rd Series, I (October 1944) and II (January 1945).

Mazzei, Philip. *Memoirs of the Life and Peregrinations of the Florentine Philip Mazzei 1730-1816*. (Translated by Howard R. Marraro.) New York: Columbia University Press (1942).

Schiavo, Giovanni. *One of America's Founding Fathers.* New York: Vigo Press (1951).

Wilstach, Paul. *Jefferson and Monticello.* New York: Doubleday, Page (1925).

CONSTANTINO BRUMIDI

Brown, Glen. *History of the United States Capitol.* Washington, D. C.: Government Printing Office (V. 1, 1900; V. 2, 1903).

Compilation of Works of Art and Other Objects in the United States Capitol. Washington, D. C.: Government Printing Office (1966).

Fairman, Charles E. "Our Debt to Italy"; "The Art of the Italian Artists in the United States Capitol." *The Congressional Record.* (Jan. 28, 1925; Jan. 29, 1930.)

Hazelton, George C. *Our National Capitol: Its Architecture, Art and History.* New York: J. F. Taylor (1914).

Herron, Paul. *The Story of Capitol Hill.* New York: Coward, McCann (1963).

Life Magazine. "The Capitol: A Picture Tour." July 2, 1951.

Martin, Edward W. *Behind the Scenes in Washington.* Continental Publishing (1873).

Moore, Joseph W. *Picturesque Washington.* Providence (1887).

Murdock, Myrtle Cheney. *Constantino Brumidi: Michelangelo of the United States Capitol.* Baltimore, Md.: Monumental Press (1950).

The Capitol: Symbol of Freedom. Washington, D. C.: Government Printing Office (1963).

LUIGI PALMA DI CESNOLA

Calvert, Henry Murray. *Reminiscences of a Boy in Blue.* 1862-1865. New York: G. Putnam's Sons (1920).

Cesnola, General Louis Palma di. *Cyprus: Its Ancient Cities, Tombs, and Temples.* New York: Harper & Bros. (1878).

———. *Ten Months in Libby Prison.* U. S. Sanitary Commission (1865).

——— (editor). *The Metropolitan Museum of Art.* New York: D. Appleton (1882).

Howe, Winifred E. *A History of the Metropolitan Museum of Art.* New York: The Metropolitan Museum of Art (V. 1, 1913; V. 2, 1946).

Myres, J. L. (editor). *Handbook of the Cesnola Collection of Antiquities from Cyprus* (1914).

Preyer, David C. *The Art of the Metropolitan Museum of New York.* Boston: Page Co. (1913).

Roversi, Luigi. *Luigi Palma di Cesnola e il Metropolitan Museum of Art di New York.* New York (1898).

SAINT FRANCES XAVIER CABRINI

Borden, Lucille Papin. *Francesca Cabrini: Without Staff or Scrip.* New York: Macmillan (1945).

Cabrini, Francesca Xavier. *Travels of Mother Frances Xavier Cabrini.* (Letters to The Missionary Sisters of the Sacred Heart, The Alumnae and Students of the Teacher's College in Rome.) Chicago, Ill.: Missionary Sisters of the Sacred Heart (1944).

Di Donato, Pietro. *Immigrant Saint: The Life of Mother Cabrini.* New York: McGraw-Hill (1960).

Maynard, Theodore. *Great Catholics in American History.* New York: Hanover House (1957).

———. *Saints for Our Times.* (St. Frances Xavier Cabrini.) New York: Appleton-Century-Crofts (1952).

———. *Too Small a World: The Life of Francesca Cabrini.* Milwaukee: Bruce Publishing Co. (1945).

Riis, Jacob. *How the Other Half Lives: Studies Among the Tenements of New York.* New York: Charles Scribner's Sons (1894).

ARTURO TOSCANINI

Antek, Samuel. *This Was Toscanini.* New York: Vanguard Press (1963).

Chotzinoff, Samuel. *Toscanini: An Intimate Portrait.* New York: Alfred A. Knopf (1956).

Ewen, David. *The Story of Arturo Toscanini.* New York: Henry Holt & Co. (1951).

Gatti-Casazza, Giulio. *Memories of the Opera.* New York: Charles Scribner's Sons (1941).

Gilman, Lawrence. *Toscanini and Great Music.* New York: Farrar & Rinehart (1938).

Haggin, B. H. *Conversations with Toscanini.* New York: Doubleday & Co. (1959).

Hughes, Spike. *The Toscanini Legacy.* London: Putnams (1959).

Kolodin, Irving. *The Story of the Metropolitan Opera, 1883-1950.* New York: Alfred A. Knopf (1953).

Sacchi, Filippo. *The Magic Baton: Toscanini's Life for Music.* New York: G. P. Putnam's Sons (1957).

Sargeant, Winthrop. *Geniuses, Goddesses and People.* New York: E. P. Dutton & Co. (1949).

Schickel, Richard. *The World of Carnegie Hall.* New York: Julian Messner, Inc. (1960).

Stefan-Gruenfeldt, Paul. *Arturo Toscanini.* (With foreword by Stefan Zweig.) New York: Viking Press (1936).

Taubman, Howard. *The Maestro: The Life of Arturo Toscanini.* New York: Simon & Schuster (1951).

A. P. GIANNINI

Dana, Julian. *A. P. Giannini—Giant in the West.* New York: Prentice-Hall (1947).

Forbes, B. C. (editor). *America's Fifty Foremost Business Leaders.* (For "L. M. Giannini," by Mark Harrison.) New York: B. C. Forbes Publishing Co. (1948).

Forbes, B. C. *Men Who Are Making the West.* New York: B. C. Forbes Publishing Co. (1923).

James, Marquis, and James, Bessie Rowland. *Biography of a Bank: The Story of Bank of America, N. T. & S. A.* New York: Harper & Bros. (1954).

Nicosia, Francesco M. *Italian Pioneers of California.* San Francisco: Italian-American Chamber of Commerce (1960).

Rink, Paul. *A. P. Giannini—Building the Bank of America.* Chicago: Encyclopaedia Britannica Press (1963).

The Bank That Makes History. Pamphlet published by the Training Department, Bank of America N. T. & S. A., San Francisco, Calif.

FIORELLO H. LA GUARDIA

Cuneo, Ernest. *Life with Fiorello.* New York: Macmillan (1955).

Franklin, Jay. *La Guardia: A Biography.* New York: Modern Age Books (1937).

Gluck, Gemma La Guardia. *My Story.* New York: David McKay Co. (1961).

La Guardia, Fiorello H. *The Making of an Insurgent: An Autobiography, 1882-1919.* (Edited by M. R. Werner.) Philadelphia: J. B. Lippincott (1948).

Limpus, Lowell, and Leyson, Burr. *This Man La Guardia.* New York: E. P. Dutton & Co. (1938).

Mann, Arthur. *La Guardia: A Fighter Against His Times 1882-1933.* Philadelphia: J. B. Lippincott (1959).

———. *La Guardia Comes to Power 1933.* Philadelphia: J. B. Lippincott (1965).

Moses, Robert. *La Guardia: A Salute and a Memoir.* New York: Simon & Schuster (1957). (Or *New York Times Magazine,* Sept. 8, 1957.)

Rodman, Bella. *Fiorello La Guardia.* (In collaboration with Philip Sterling.) New York: Hill and Wang (1962).

Tugwell, Rexford Guy. *The Art of Politics: As Practiced by Three Great Americans.* New York: Doubleday & Co. (1958).

Weidman, Jerome, and Abbott, George. *Fiorello!* (A musical comedy based on La Guardia's early career in politics.) New York: Random House (1960).

Weston, Paul B. *A Hammer in the City.* (Biography of La Guardia). Evanston, Illinois: Regency Books (1962).

ENRICO FERMI

Amrine, Michael. *The Great Decision: The Secret History of the Atomic Bomb.* New York: G. P. Putnam's Sons (1959).

Bulletin of the Atomic Scientists. January 1955. (Tributes at memorial service for Enrico Fermi.)

Compton, Arthur H. *Atomic Quest.* New York: Oxford University Press (1956).

Fermi, Laura. *Atoms in the Family: My Life with Enrico Fermi.* Chicago: University of Chicago Press (1954).

———. *The Story of Atomic Energy.* New York: Random House, Inc. Landmark Books (1961).

Giovannitti, Len, and Freed, Fred. *The Decision to Drop the Bomb.* New York: Coward-McCann (1965).

Groves, Leslie R. *Now It Can Be Told: The Story of the Manhattan Project.* New York: Harper & Bros. (1962).

Jungk, Robert. *Brighter Than a Thousand Suns: Personal History of the Atomic Scientists.* New York: Harcourt, Brace & Co. (1958).

Lang, Daniel. *From Hiroshima to the Moon: Chronicles of Life in the Atomic Age.* New York: Simon & Schuster (1959).

Lamont, Lansing. *Day of Trinity.* New York: Atheneum (1965).

Lapp, Ralph E. *Atoms and People.* New York: Harper & Bros. (1956).

———. *Roads to Discovery.* New York: Harper & Bros. (1960).

Laurence, William L. *Dawn Over Zero: The Story of the Atomic Bomb.* New York: Alfred Knopf (1946).

———. *Men and Atoms: The Discovery, the Uses and the Future of Atomic Energy.* New York: Simon & Schuster (1959).

Purcell, John. *The Best-Kept Secret: The Story of the Atomic Bomb.* New York: Vanguard Press (1963).

Rasetti, Franco. "Enrico Fermi." *Science,* April 1955.

Smyth, Henry DeWolf. *Atomic Energy for Military Purposes.* The Official Report on the Development of the Atomic Bomb under the Auspices of the U. S. Government 1940-1945. Princeton, N. J.: Princeton University Press (1945).

Index